The Gist

A Celebration of the Imagination

Edited by
Lindsay Clarke

In association with
Lorna Howarth – The Write Factor
and Ruth Borthwick – Arvon

First published in 2012
by The Write Factor
in association with Arvon

www.thewritefactor.co.uk
www.arvonfoundation.org

ISBN 978-0-9568735-2-1

A CIP catalogue record for this book is available from the British Library.

Cover Image: Great Eastern Sun by John Moat
Designed and typeset by Simon Willby
Printed by Imprint Digital

In Acknowledgement of the Work of

John Moat

"... The outer world and inner world are interdependent at every moment. We are simply the locus of their collision. Two worlds, with mutually contradictory laws, or laws that seem to us to be so, colliding afresh at every second, struggling for peaceful co-existence. And whether we like it or not our life is what we are able to make out of that collision and struggle. So what we need, evidently, is a faculty that embraces both worlds simultaneously... and which pays equal respects to both sides. Which keeps faith, as Goethe says, with the world of things and the world of spirits equally. This really is Imagination."

Ted Hughes, *Myth and Education*, 1976

CONTENTS

Editor's Note   11
Preface RUTH BORTHWICK   15
Foreword ANDREW MOTION   17
The Gist of Arvon JOHN MOAT   19

IMAGES

Two Poems CAROL ANN DUFFY   37
Mythic Imagination JULES CASHFORD   41
Diary of a Wind Poem ALICE OSWALD   55
Visitations SEAMUS HEANEY   61
The Project ANDREW MILLER   73
Lured Into the Light: The Voice of the Poet ADAM THORPE   77
Sixteens LAWRENCE SAIL   91
Adventures in the Underworld LINDSAY CLARKE   97
Two Poems COLETTE BRYCE   109
Secret Fire PATRICK HARPUR   113
The Sweet Voice of Reason LINDA PROUD   123
A Place of Constant Surprises NICK STIMSON   133

RECOLLECTIONS

Memories of Arvon PENELOPE SHUTTLE   145
Five Days MAGGIE GEE   149
My Life at Totleigh Barton MONIQUE ROFFEY   155
A Hand of Friendship and a Heart of Love SATISH KUMAR   165

Appendix: Arvon and Education TED HUGHES   173

RESPONSES   185

Afterthought: Unfinished Business? JOHN MOAT   211

The Contributors   217

THE TWO JOHNS &
THE STORY OF THIS BOOK

THIS COLLECTION OF essays, poems and reflections has been assembled in recognition of the life and work of an extraordinary man who prefers, on the whole, not to draw attention to himself. For that reason it is offered principally, as John Moat would wish, in celebration of the Imagination; and – whatever else it may be – *The Gist* is evidence that when plans go awry and life gets hard, the Imagination can always come up with something new.

John and I were supposed to tutor an Arvon course entitled *Mythic Imagination* at The Hurst in June 2012, with our friend Jules Cashford as guest reader. As it turned out, life had other ideas and it became necessary to cancel the course, which felt sad all round. However, out of the imagining consequent upon that disappointment emerged the idea for this book. As is customary at Arvon, sixteen participants would have come to the course, so we have gathered sixteen contributing writers here, and readers might like to think of what follows as a virtual Arvon course with two presiding tutors: John Moat (whose essay *The Gist of Arvon* provides the starting point) and his dear friend and co-founder of Arvon, the late John Fairfax.

John Moat is a man for whom I have enormous admiration and

respect – as a poet, novelist, painter, humourist, educator, activist and benefactor. I also hold him in great affection as a friend, so it has been a real pleasure to bring this book together in honour of his accomplishments. Sadly, I wasn't lucky enough to know John Fairfax, but another important purpose of this book is to recognise his vital part in what was a remarkable collaboration.

Writing of their joint efforts, John Moat said that "the earliest determination of Arvon was something indivisibly shared by the two Johns, and it's been suggested that it was as much the merriment as the trust and shared reckless compulsion in their working together that informed the blood of Arvon from the outset." In conceiving Arvon and nurturing its growth, each of the two friends brought his own talent to what was shared. John Moat tells me that while he was "more the strategist in matters of enablement, funding and extending the application of Arvon," John Fairfax was "the secure anchor-man, insisting that any development must relate directly and uncompromisingly back to Arvon's founding principle."

Both the form they devised together for Arvon courses and the convivial character they gave to them have endured successfully over so many years that it's clear we are paying tribute here to *two* remarkable men – two poets, as distinguished by their visionary powers of Imagination as by the loyalty of their long friendship. So, as well as a pleasure, it has been a privilege to help to shape a book which, in spirit and intention, rejoices in their extraordinary shared achievement.

But there is a woman to be acknowledged here too. Antoinette Moat has been John's wife, muse, help-meet, support, companion, co-conspirator and colleague in their many enterprises throughout the years (she single-handedly furnished and equipped Totleigh Barton and, to a large extent, Lumb Bank and so set the essential Arvon atmosphere of 'at home') and I'm sure John would be the first to admit how much of his own creativity as writer, artist and activist is attributable to her strength, intelligence and sensitivity. Marriage too is a collaborative endeavour and theirs has been a long and happy one. This book truly belongs to the two of them.

My thanks are due to Carol Hughes for her kind permission to reprint Ted Hughes' still powerfully prescient essay on the educational importance of Arvon, and to Andrew Motion for his generous Foreword. But this book could not have happened at all were it not for the enthusiastic support of Ruth Borthwick and the Trustees of Arvon, for the cheerful, voluntary efforts of John Moat's publisher, Lorna Howarth of The Write Factor, in overseeing its production. I owe a huge debt of thanks to them and also to Simon Willby for his skillful work in designing such a beautiful edition..

Most of all, however, I want to express my heartfelt thanks to each of the contributing writers who, under the pressure of a risibly short deadline, gave so liberally of their talents and time to light up the following pages in lively celebration of the Imagination.

Lindsay Clarke

PREFACE

IT IS AN extraordinary privilege to work for an organisation whose sole purpose is to enable people's creativity. At Arvon we believe that everyone can be a writer and this is at the core of everything we do. It seems to me that this matters more than ever today at a moment when the opportunity for many of us to find time and space to develop our Imagination – particularly young and disadvantaged people – is under threat. John Moat and John Fairfax's project seems even more radical in this context. This book is offered in that spirit.

Lindsay Clarke is central to this project. It was his idea and he has ushered it into life with a light touch to which our writers have responded with verve. He has worked tirelessly with Lorna Howarth of The Write Factor, John's neighbour and publisher, to make this book happen. On Arvon's behalf I thank them and am humbled by them.

All the writers have given their work freely and Arvon is indebted to them for their generosity. Thank you so much. You are Arvon.

Finally, I want to say a huge thank you to John Moat for his unswerving support to the Arvon project. My heart lifts when I hear his warm greeting on the phone, usually on a Friday afternoon, when my energy may be flagging. He is a constant and joyful source of inspiration. As I say, I am lucky.

Ruth Borthwick
Chief Executive
Arvon

FOREWORD

ARVON IS ONE of this country's most vital signs of literary life, and John Moat has been, together with his close friend the poet John Fairfax, its prime mover and durable inspiration. This has required a degree of devotion that is itself remarkable. Just as extraordinary is the fine balance he has managed to strike, in order to make everything work so well. On the one hand, Arvon exists to teach the craft of writing, to unravel merely obfuscating mysteries, and to explore the benefits of calm commitment. On the other hand, it creates the largest plausible space in which a free spirit can discover its freedom, in which difficulties can be explored as well as resolved, in which writers can go to the edge of themselves in order to find the centre of themselves.

A sense of adventure? Certainly: that is what the Arvon courses pioneered and continue to allow, because they encourage sense and adventure to combine. John's friends know that he possesses these qualities himself, and his readers see them mingling in his poems as well. But to have helped in such a crucial way to body them forth in a Foundation – that is another marvellous achievement. It means that every year hundreds of people (without perhaps knowing this is the case) are inspired by his example. It also means the whole landscape of literature is continually illuminated without becoming garish, and made hospitable without losing its necessary excitement.

Andrew Motion

THE GIST OF ARVON

John Moat

MORE THAN FORTY years since Fairfax and I made the move that would lead to the setting up of Arvon. From the start it was the idea that knew where it was headed. In fact it often seemed that the idea had simply requisitioned us – we were primed as operatives, but would act reliably only if kept well away from the controls. In truth, I suppose at the outset we *had* had a bit of an idea: that it would be good to create a space where individuals, and in particular young committed writers, could be given a sanctuary away from, as we saw it, the creative deprivation imposed by the system of standard education – and there offered what the pair of us had been gifted, the guidance of experienced writers. But then the idea itself took over and we were left to act like a couple of sorcerer's apprentices, watching in amazement as the spell constantly came up with the goods. Apparently it also conferred on us a magic agency – we needed only to say the word to a person to find the idea had infected them. And the result of that was/has been/is a national organisation with headquarters in London and four regional centres which over the years have employed getting on for 2,000 writers to work with many thousands of individuals eager to explore their own gift for writing.

I've often wondered to what extent the thrust behind the adventure came from Fairfax and myself and how much was the determination of the Imagination itself? Most of us use the word Imagination without worrying that we haven't a clue to what it means. What it means to us, or what it means to anyone. Most often it's used to relate to an individual's creativity – to his or her originality (whatever that means!) and inventiveness. To some it is a gift, like the ability to dowse; to some it is more of an aptitude, like being clever; to some it is nothing less than the conveyance of the highest truth. But thinking of it in relation to Arvon I've wondered whether it isn't a formative force, universally inclusive, and which the Player King in Hamlet has a brave shot at describing when he says, "Our thoughts are ours, their ends none of our own." And that has led me to wonder further how failure to grasp how this formative, determining mystery, properly reverenced, is the guide and unfolding force in the lives and ventures of every individual, and their society, and above all their education, amounts to a serious 'missing of the mark'. One that leaves individuals and society, to use a current phrase, unfit for purpose.

If the concern of the Imagination is universal, how come we individuals can get the impression that its focus is exclusively on us, or even on so small a detail as one of our ventures? Maybe because if we allow the Imagination to become involved, then the venture is informed by universal concern… or *intention*. But how does the Imagination become involved? Is it always to hand, waiting for an opportunity; or is the opportunity something it engineers itself?

I trace the first seed-sprout of Arvon, my part in it at least, back to when I was six. I'd been exposed to poetry, Irish mostly (my mother's doing), and could recite Kipling's *The Cells* and *Gunga Din* (probably my father's doing, he'd been in the Indian Army). I was working on a poem – that's how I remember it – a serious ballad to commemorate my father being killed in battle in Malaya the year before. If the endeavour was precocious it was as nothing compared to the precociousness of my frustration at being unable to bring it to life. I think now that the frustration was in part at my being unable to realise the intention, but also because I was failing to meet the expectation of my father.

What expectation? I had barely known him, but my mother's determination to install me with a manly role-model had made of him an idealised character, remote, unfeeling and as judgemental as God the Father Almighty. It was to take me half a lifetime to acknowledge that in the flesh he was a man I would have got on with, in fact have – as had so many others – loved very much. But the unfounded expectation went to work on me, and being unfounded it was something I could never conceivably realise. I can see now that it was like being suddenly locked into a form of non-existence – and there the Imagination could no longer reach me. This empty world was regulated from outside by an authoritarian and abstract book of precept – which in due course came fully into its own at two all-male boarding schools – and in this world I was subject to the same unfounded expectations which conditioned me to accepting I would be at best an indifferent performer. In truth, the Imagination did still occasionally come knocking – but for all this impact of reality I viewed the visits as urgently secret, probably shameful, and at any cost to be hidden from the patriarchal legislature.

Anything familiar about this? Yes, of course. You don't require the loss of a father to have been suddenly expelled from the magical domain where the child is at home into the cold confinement of standard education. My experience is merely a metaphor for what in our society is experienced by almost all of us – almost anyone who has been to school, or encouraged by ambitious, or just devoted parents, concerned we should succeed in the *real* world.

We marvel at the way children create their own worlds, and seem impelled to make images, drawings, paintings of these realms – their stories, delights, horrors – with effortless, spontaneous, innocent engagement. We may even momentarily register that each creation is authentic, being both universal and unique – and as such a little unschooled testament to the supreme mystery of the Many and the One. But then don't we shrug our shoulders in blank acceptance when overnight the child's spontaneity and engagement is lost, the light gone out, overtaken by the glare of common day? Except in those few of us whose concordance with the Imagination is in-built, somehow indomitable.

Maybe I was, or could have been, one of these. Maybe the occasions in the ten school-years following that initial withdrawal when, always on my own, the Imagination in full colour would momentarily take me off-guard, were precise 'trailers' to what would happen one night when I was fifteen. It was the holidays. I was sleeping in my bedroom at home. I woke – came suddenly awake – in the small hours to find the light on in my room. Startled, I sat up in bed. I looked around. The familiarity of the room was unfamiliar. In a mirror on the wall opposite I caught sight of myself, startled, apparently listening intently. And the light began to die, slowly went out of the room. I've wondered what would ever have happened if I'd shrugged my shoulders and gone back to sleep. But that wasn't to be the way of it. I switched on the light, went down into the silent house, and came back with a sketch-pad and pastels belonging to my stepfather. And then I made a little picture of what I had seen in the mirror. A lad sitting up in bed, his expression startled, attentive, wondering. When I'd finished it occurred to me he'd perhaps heard an intruder in the house. I wrote a title beneath: 'Who's there?'

It was twenty-five years before I came alive to that title's two-level significance – and began to wonder whether the answer to the question were not the boy who nine years before had been left in the dark.

So what was the light? Had the light returned? Or resurfaced? And what did it amount to? The truth is, it wasn't a bad picture (I sold it later for ten bob to a member of the Cricket XI who fancied my sister). I took it back to school, and on a day, sure that there was no one else around, in a sweat of apprehension, I sneaked to the Art Room. The Art Master, who like so many art teachers, (praise be!) was known to be a commanding free spirit, was there on his own. A deep breath, and I showed him the painting. He looked at me, and then looked at the painting a few seconds through narrowed eyes, and then looked at me again – this time more of a passing glance as he handed back the picture and walked away. "Can't think why you don't do more," he said.

And that was enough? Enough for the Imagination to work with. The way was open, even if from the outset the operation has always needed to be covert – away from the glare of his certainty (whoever *he* happens to be). In my little book *The Founding of Arvon* I detail how a way, inconceivable before this visitation, unfolded without any recourse to logic until it included my being fetched with Fairfax to hold the door open for Arvon itself.

Within three months of leaving school I was, by unlikely appointment, working in France with the painter Edmond Kapp. It was he who first had me admit to, and then encouraged, my need to write. By the end of the year he had introduced me to his old friend David Higham, one of the country's most eminent literary agents, who read a small book I'd written and invited me to be 'on his books'. There followed four charmed years at Oxford (details of how I came to be admitted is something the Authorities to this day would probably choose to suppress) with Nevill Coghill and Jonathan Wordsworth for tutors, and ending with a respectable but totally unwarranted degree. Then came an attempt at full-time writing which I only narrowly survived, but which led to my undertaking a form of apprenticeship with the South African poet, John Howland Beaumont. Then to the collision with Fairfax in the pub; to Antoinette who introduced a little sanity; to a novel published… and thence to Arvon.

If I'm suggesting that Arvon wouldn't have come into being but for the experience with the light in my bedroom, and that the experience and the unfolding of it that followed were related to the Imagination, I've come close to claiming that the Imagination carries an *intention*. Then I'd better own what this would seem to infer – that whatever mystery the Imagination amounts to, the field of its operation reaches beyond the individual creativity we usually connect it with. Reaches beyond it, and is *wholly* concerned with it. It has the capacity to relate the individual to the universal, and would seem *intent* on enabling the individual by expressing him or herself to realise that the unique story they have to tell is essential to the completion of the all-inclusive story of the universe.

So here's the bottom line: there is an existential onus on each individual "to know thyself" – to tell his or her own story (and this in no way relates exclusively to writing, nor the fine arts, but to the story as told by the self-expressive act or utterance or enactment of *every* individual). The full of this can be achieved only through recourse to the Imagination: to provide guidance and opportunity for this to happen must, one would have thought, be the primary concern of genuine education. And what my own experience brought home to me is that where the mystery with its *intention* (which here is focused on the self-realisation or fulfilment of the individual) is overridden by some extraneous intention, the individual is cut off from the Imagination – and his or her story is suspended. This means that any situation (which includes every *human* situation) whose health is dependent on the realised potential of the individuals involved, must be compromised by a system that marginalises the immanent reality of the Imagination. To call such a system 'educational' is, to say the least, a misnomer.

This morning I hear on the radio a government Minister for

Education say that it is the responsibility of the 'System' to ensure that every child achieves his or her potential. That sounds fine... until overtaken by the chilling thought, "And by whose criteria will this potential be defined? Or processed? Or evaluated?" After all, an individual's potential that relates to their ability to contribute on behalf of society to rising living standards, wider consumer choice and survival in the cut-throat global economy, may not be the same as that which, when realised, would contribute to the city culture William Blake had in mind for England's green and pleasant land! The capacity to be open and responsive to the Imagination is every child's, every individual's most precious gift. When that gift is realised, i.e. when the individual has thus uniquely expressed him or herself, then this is the unique gift that each has to offer. Surely then it is the gift that society, and if not society, then you and I, should do most to protect?

If this were true maybe we should be wondering what is the outlook for a society that regards the Imagination as a handy aptitude of a minority of its population – one that can be schooled and harnessed to productive citizenship, and employed to maximise GNP. It wouldn't be a big surprise to learn that the government of such a society was focusing its support for the arts on something called 'The Arts as Industry'. The educational system of this society would serve its priorities – in order to hone the population to maximum production it must impose standard grades, abstract targets, and its own full-time prescribed curriculum. Individual self-expression, and teachers with experience and time to guide their students, would be surplus to necessity.

Control – attribute of the rational mind and the male disposition: precisely the force that dominates the government of virtually every nation. Behind the need to control is the fear of being out of control, and of forces 'beyond our control'. Hence the tendency for control endlessly to modify itself in a drive for total control. And there's nothing so powers the drive as the constant dark presentiment that the better half of life is beyond control. Feeling for instance, which the rational mind dismisses as the register of the unreliable feminine (but which it will have to learn to embrace if it is ever to achieve balance) – and the uncontrollable one who communicates almost exclusively through feeling, i.e. the Imagination. At the back of the class, probably hugging the radiator and reading a novel, there'll always be one or two who don't do dates and sums, and are by constitution unresponsive to their schooling. Fairfax and I for instance. So when our paths, or a covert *intention*, landed us under the guidance of poets who had learned their trade in a different school, we were readily 'radicalised'. It was what we took from these teachers that we drew on when finally we were requisitioned by the idea of Arvon.

Let's say, four things. First, we'd now experienced how with any art or craft it is only the living and practice of it that provides the authority that can offer someone else genuine guidance. Those who live the practice then carry the experience with them, and become its embodiment, a part of their presence – which is why a mere encounter can be a form of guidance. My first meeting with Edmond Kapp, which was also my first encounter with a wholly dedicated artist, lasted no more than forty minutes, and yet by the end I knew I had undergone radical alteration. Not only had a door with my name on it been opened, but I was through it – I hadn't a clue where I'd fetched up, but knew there was no going back. Later, an encounter with John Howland Beaumont provided more specific guidance – he was a writer and poet. Fairfax had had a similar experience with his uncle, the poet George Barker. Which is why we needed no discussion – the only people we would ask to be tutors must be experienced imaginative writers.

Second, was having it demonstrated that the Imagination is, or is part of, an unguarded generosity. Any endeavour sanctioned by the Imagination will, if true to itself, be proof of this in heart, word and deed. Not by the requisite mission statement printed under your logo, but in spirit pervasive as oxygen in the bloodstream. And so unavoidably *inclusive*. Our mentors, by being fully available and committed to guiding us in our attempts to make of ourselves a way for the Imagination, put this generosity on the line – though they made the proviso quite clear that this was on the understanding that their commitment was chiefly to the Imagination itself, and would extend to us for so long as our own commitment and willingness to practice the craft matched their own. Important this, because it should be stressed that no one hereabouts is offering the easy or otiose option, or that genuine education will not involve hard work, discipline and the mastering of relevant skills.

This then was the role we suggested to those we asked to tutor. None needed instruction. They were attracted to the situation we were offering them, and even though the fee was very small, were eager to take part; and I now feel that an eagerness to teach, or act mentor, is most often an attribute of realised imaginative authority – and that this authority extends in individual style to the ability to offer guidance. Each in his or her own way gave themselves to the venture. With the exception of the very few who over the years have missed the mark and come to teach at Arvon out of regard for themselves, tutors (that's getting on for two thousand of them) have been giving ever since.

If it's true that generosity is a feature of the creative Imagination, it would seem obvious why the prevailing system of education should generally ignore it: the 'system' doesn't do business with generosity. In fact quite the opposite – it is openly extortionate. Teachers for the most are, or would be, generous – but not the system. If it gives, it gives only on condition that it will be repaid, and with interest. It provides for and rewards not in relation to individual potential, but in so far as the individual meets its demands. And to earn even this small favour he or she is made to compete... cut-throat competition with their brothers, sisters, friends and every other candidate for a place on the ladder to... to material success. A sound, pragmatic policy this for a nation involved in cut-throat competition with fellow nations for survival in the global marketplace. The system is thorough, systematically exclusive and as draconian as the celebrated bed of Procrustes... except if you fail the test, you won't be cut down to size – you'll simply be excluded.

The Imagination on the other hand runs an 'open door' policy and is universally inclusive, and the wealth it promises is fulfilment. From the outset, Arvon's tutors have been the surety, (or is it the medium?) of this generosity. And Arvon's enduring success is because the generosity has somehow embraced everyone who has contributed to the Arvon adventure: council members, staff, friends and above all, in their openness and eagerness, those who come on the courses.

Third, that the Imagination, whether it visits us in the thunder or in the still, small voice, commands an undivided attention; is most likely to engage with us when, even in company, we are alone. To paraphrase St Paul, we can be taught to speak with the tongues of men and of angels, but to speak with our own voice, to avoid becoming another member of the tinkling cymbal section of our primary, secondary, university education, we must at some point find ourselves unimpededly open to, and one to one with the emptiness that is the storeroom of the Imagination. Fairfax and I felt that to provide opportunity for some such encounter should be integral to an Arvon course – which is why we suggested that the second day in the four-day course should give students the chance to be alone, while providing support and a safe place for what many who come from a world of habitual busy-ness, might find a quite daunting adventure.

No such provision of course in the system's current crammed

curricula of teachers, teacher-trainees or students. But it's worth recalling that at the outset of Arvon forty years ago, teacher-training colleges included in their programmes an Activities Week during which students could explore some creative discipline outside their syllabus. Sometimes this gap in the curriculum would achieve the opening we planned for with Day 2 of an Arvon course. The success of the courses Arvon ran for teacher-trainees was key to its early survival – but it also extended our understanding of Arvon's potential. The quality of the work produced, and which in many cases the trainees continued to produce, remains haunting evidence of the untapped store of talent among today's teachers. It almost certainly also suggests why there are so many teachers unfulfilled and demoralised when their workload and the bureaucratic demands leave them no opportunity for creative contact with the Imagination. We have to realise that this system of education fails society when it denies teachers such experience that would not only enrich their lives, but afford them authority to nurture the imaginative life of their students. This failure devalues the vocation of the teacher – and in direct contradiction of the government's aims, is compromising the creative potential of the country.

Fourth, and hardest to get word to, is an essence that work with those experienced writers brought home to us. Maybe the word is one not much in fashion: reverence. Reverence for what quantum scientists might call the *intentionality* of the venture. Robert Frost in his poem *Two Tramps in Mudtime* comes as close to expressing this intentionality as is ever likely to be possible in a single statement:

> Only where love and need are one,
> And work is play for mortal stakes
> Is the deed ever really done
> For Heaven and the future's sakes.

Here, for me at least, are implied the qualities that render radical the approach to education that Arvon identifies with: Inclusiveness, Rigour, Light-heartedness. Oh, and Sincerity. The four, in sum, amount to Reverence.

The word sincerity is used by Zen Buddhists to describe the spirit of good practice. Shunryu Suzuki in his fine introduction to meditation, *Zen Mind, Beginner's Mind*, writes, "You should get rid of excessive things – if your practice is good, without being aware of it you will become proud of your practice. That pride is extra. What you do is good, but something more is added to it. You should get rid of that something that is extra. This point is very, very important, but usually we are not subtle enough to realise it, and we go in the wrong direction." Self-expressive work, informed by the Imagination, is, *in the making*, an end it itself. In the making there can be no secondary concerns, nothing *in order that* – and for an initiative that exists to fortify the imaginative self-expression of individuals this means that concern with the achievement of recognition, success in the market, enhanced academic performance, increased self-confidence (all of which Arvon could justifiably point to) are *something extra*. At best they are secondary, or merely incidental. And yet often because these are measurable results, they impress potential funders – and then to feature them can become a temptation. But were they ever to become the primary concern, the *something extra* would have taken over. Arvon would have lost its way – or at least lost touch with its origin.

So too has a society that views the Imagination as utilitarian – as useful only when concerned with *something extra* – lost its way. Why, you might expect such a society to be one that viewed Nature as a resource to be exploited, or the Arts as a process of profitable industry, or Education as the efficient supply line of productive citizens. It would be a society that for its convenience had alienated itself from its essential livelihood, and turned its back on the creative potential of its humanity. In which case Arvon's little adventure (and there are many out there not unlike it) would be as that of the tumbler W.B.Yeats told of, who laid out his mat in the path of the advancing army – simply witness to what might be otherwise.

Ask for a quote that speaks of the Imagination and most often you'll be referred to Shakespeare's,

> And as imagination bodies forth
> The forms of things unknown, the poet's pen
> Turns them to shapes, and gives to airy nothing
> A local habitation and a name.

What on earth do we take that to mean? What on earth does the Minister of Education take it to mean? And yet everyone who has ever been fingered by the Imagination must have felt in their marrow they are included in something that goes beyond them, that they have been able to offer a local habitation and give a name to it, and so be part of some mysterious intentionality. When the painter whose studio Don Quixote visits is asked what he is painting and he replies, "That is as it may turn out to be"; or when recently Anthony Gormley says that "Art is an individual observing his or her own experience"; or when fifty-five years ago the boy, after the strange light has withdrawn from his bedroom, goes down into the dark house in search of a sketchbook; or when the lad just returned from the first Arvon course writes, "We had been called upon to write as if writing mattered... I think what was shattering was that suddenly everything mattered," – each is alive to what is *bodying forth*.

* * *

Alpha, the beginning. Here is the intention: to arrive at the beginning and to know the place for the first time. Omega, the ultimate coming home. Alpha and Omega – the beginning and the end of the Story.

The scintilla of enlightenment that illuminates every imaginative act or presentiment or work of art – every realised moment of imaginative self-expression, yields a clearer view of home.

Arvon has always thought of its Centres as both writing houses and homes. At the outset we told tutors to think of the Centre as their home, which *they* had opened to their students, and so it was *homely* for the students to be part of the cooking and the skills in running the home. Arvon still insists on the importance of this, on keeping away from any feel of an institution – and accepts that making home is appropriate provision and metaphor for an imaginative enterprise.

People, time and again, say that their experience of coming to Arvon is like being allowed home. John Fairfax, who died at home in his Thatched Cottage, wrote in a poem, 'To grow a man must love his home.'

"Only where love and need..." Love... What's love got to do with it? What's love got to do with the Imagination? Ask William Blake: "Eternity is in love with the productions of time." Ask Henri Matisse: "But is not love the origin of all creation?"

In the end the only context one has to work with is oneself. So the mystery of the Imagination is apparent to me only in what I take to be those mysterious synchronicities and appointments that have shaped and *directed* my experience – until now, as I grow old and mystery seems somehow more immediate, I find a quickening sense not only of my life being something imagined, but as being individually party to *the* Imagining; and – just as everyone else's unique life is – essential to its completeness. To what end? I don't know, but will make do with Omega – perhaps even settle for Teilhard de Chardin's *Omega Point* which is, if I understand him, the universal realisation of Love.

That then's the gist of it: of why Arvon values and seeks to nourish individual Imagination. That, for as long as it exists and is in touch with its own beginnings, is the gist of Arvon.

IMAGES

TWO POEMS

Carol Ann Duffy

These poems were written while tutoring at Arvon centres. The first was written at Totleigh Barton, the second at Moniack Mhor.

Miles Away

I want you and you are not here, I pause
in this garden, breathing the colour thought is
before language into still air. Even your name
is a pale ghost and, though I exhale it again
and again, it will not stay with me. Tonight
I make you up, imagine you, your movements clearer
than the words I have you say you said before.

Wherever you are now, inside my head you fix me
with a look, standing here whilst cool late light
dissolves into the earth. I have got your mouth wrong,
but still it smiles. I hold you closer, miles away,
inventing love, until the calls of nightjars
interrupt and turn what was to come, was certain,
into memory. The stars are filming us for no one.

Moniack Mhor

Something is dealing from a deck of cards,
face up, seven, a week of mornings, today's
revealing the hills at Moniack Mhor, shrugging off
their mists. A sheepdog barks six fields away;
I see the farm from here.

Twelve-month cards, each one thumbed, flipped,
weathered in its way – this the eighth, harvest-time,
a full moon like a trump, a magic trick.
It rose last night above this house, affirmative.
I sensed your answer – hearts.

Or a single hour is a smiling Jack, a diamond,
or a spade learning a grave; charms or dark lessons.
Something is shuffling; the soft breath of Moniack Mhor
on the edge of utterance, I know it, the verbs of swifts
riffling the air

and the road turning itself into the loch, a huge ace
into which everything folds. Here is the evening,
displayed then dropped to drift to the blazon of barley, bracken,
heather. Something is gifting this great gold gathering of cloud;
a continual farewell.

MYTHIC IMAGINATION

JULES CASHFORD

AN OLD IRISH Fairy Tale tells how Fionn, the son of Uail, was set wandering in great distress of mind through Faery. Over days and nights he had many adventures, and when he returned to the world of men he was able to remember them all. In his version of the story, James Stephens says, "that by itself is wonderful, for there are few people who remember that they have been to Faery or aught of all that happened to them in that state. In truth we do not go to Faery, we become Faery, and in the beating of a pulse we may live for a year or a thousand years. But when we return the memory is quickly clouded, and we seem to have had a dream or seen a vision, although we have verily been in Faery. It was wonderful, then, that Fionn should have remembered all that happened to him in that wide-spun moment."

If we condense this narrative into an image of a state of mind we have a story of a moment of Imagination: the departure from the known, the encounter with the new and strange, the becoming one with what is found, and the re-membering, the putting together of the vision into a new whole. And what happens to us when we hear what happened to Fionn is that we also are set wandering away from the world of men, that is, from the literal frame of mind in which limits are set and predictions can be made; and, far from this world, we must become Fionn who has become Faery and, like him, we must hold the 'wide-spun' moment before our eyes.

The tale asks us to participate in two worlds simultaneously: the eternal world of Faery, where all things are possible, and Fionn's world: a man like us who has finally to return to life in time. The wonder of the tale will depend on our being able to hold both worlds together without sacrificing one to the other. William Blake called this 'double vision':

> For double the vision my eyes do see,
> And a double vision is always with me.
> With my inward eye, 'tis an old man grey,
> With my outward, a thistle across my way.

The inward and outward eye – these might seem to be two ways of seeing, two eyes, but for Blake this is one act: it is a seeing and a feeling together, seeing the thistle so intensely that he feels its inward nature, so that the vision of the old man grey comes from his feeling for the sparse, grey spikiness of the thistle. We could even say that the image of the old man grey is the image of his feeling for the thistle, an image born of the identity between them which dissolves the difference between people and plants, spirit and matter. There is a union of what those of 'Single Vision and Newton's Sleep' would separate into two things and turn back into one. But the old man grey cannot replace the thistle, because without the thistle the old man grey is no more and, in the exactness of Blake's perception, if the thistle is not felt for it is hardly seen, if seen at all:

> The tree which moves some to tears of joy is in the eyes
> of others only a green thing that stands in the way...
> But to the eyes of the man of Imagination, Nature is
> Imagination itself. As a man is, so he sees.

Because of this relation between being and seeing, Imagination cannot be treated as a separate faculty or function of the mind, which thinks in images.

We use the term 'Imagination' in many varied and imprecise ways, often indistinguishable from day-dream, fantasy, fancy, even illusion, and it is easy to forget that throughout history those who were closest to Imagination – poets, artists and visionaries – have believed it to be the deepest and sometimes the only source of knowledge. This knowledge exacts a total commitment, in contrast to knowledge gained by reasoning alone which is knowledge *about* something, not knowledge which changes you or which you have to change to know.

We have lost the simplicity of this distinction, but in Greek the term for knowing mathematics, *episteme,* was quite different from the term for knowing a person, *gnosis,* from which the Gnostics took their name – and this is the way imaginative truth is won: through relationship, love and inspiration.

Jung and James Hillman, like Blake, Coleridge and Yeats, also reinstate Imagination as the origin and ground of life. When Jung writes that "Psyche is image" and Hillman says that "All existence is structured by imagination" they are calling for a 'poetic basis of mind,' and so implicitly inviting us to see poets as psychologists, as of course they have always been. But a conclusion which follows from their work is that the language of the poets – the subtle and tacit use of image, symbol, metaphor and, still subtler, pause, rhythm, placing, tone – can bring us closer to the reality of the psyche than that other, more direct way of talking – through concept, statement and amplifying idea. For without the bewildering presence of an image we might be tempted to explain what is irrevocably mysterious.

Imagination, or the Poetic Genius, Coleridge writes, "brings the whole soul of man into activity," and requires, therefore, that the whole soul of man be brought into activity to understand it, for anything less than this is in some part an abstraction, and so untrue. Even "cold philosophy," as Shakespeare puts it, is suspect to the poet. And Yeats writes that he "thought that whatever of philosophy has been made poetry is alone permanent."

It is difficult to talk about the Imagination conceptually since we are by definition far from it when we talk *about* it. It is, perhaps, a power so ultimate that only images can call it forth, so we have, in a sense, to ask the Imagination to imagine itself. Images of fire, lightning, breath, wind and wind-harps, as well as the angels, fairies and other winged creatures, are all images which have in some moment tried to capture the elusive, invisible, fleeting, magical or divine power that we call Imagination, and whose inaccessibility to our ordinary understanding is already contained in the tantalising nature of our images of it. What else is the story of Prometheus who stole "bright-faced fire" from the gods and gave to mortals a divine privilege for which he was punished, and whose punishment reflects the wound of our opening into a sacred realm? Aeschylus has Prometheus tell how he found men witless and made them masters of their minds. He taught them how to build houses and work in wood, to distinguish the seasons and calculate the motions of the stars, to use the power of numbers, and combine letters as a means of remembering things. He taught them how to cure ills, how to consult oracles and read the meaning of dreams. "All arts that mortals have," he says, "come from Prometheus."

The range of Prometheus' gifts, their detailed and practical application, tell us that Imagination is not only for poets, or perhaps, more precisely, reminds us that the origin of the word and idea of 'poetry' lies in the Greek *poesis*, which means 'making.' Imagination, then, divines the essence in anything, transforming whatever it lights upon into art. It is a way of knowing, which is also a way of being.

Mnemosune, whose name becomes Mnemosyne in English, was the Greek goddess of Memory. This is the Orphic Hymn to her, written down between 300 BC to 300 AD:

> Mnemosune I call, the Queen, consort of Zeus,
> Mother of the sacred, holy and sweet-voiced Muses.
> Ever alien to her is evil oblivion that harms the mind,
> she holds all things together in the same dwelling place,
> in the mind and soul of mortals,
> she strengthens the powerful ability of humans to think.
> Most sweet, vigilant, she reminds us of all the thoughts
> we are for ever storing in our hearts,
> overlooking nothing, rousing each one to consciousness.
> Blessed goddess, awaken for the initiates the memory
> of the sacred rite, and banish forgetfulness from them.

We can already see that Mnemosune is a more comprehensive idea than our Memory. To start with, she is a goddess, suggesting that she is imagined as an active agent with a mind and powers of her own. Here the Cosmos itself is imagined as a living being having memory, and this memory could not be otherwise than a memory of the whole. This suggests, in turn, that the archetype of human memory is the memory of our origins, the sacred memory of the source – what Yeats calls the Great Memory. The figure of Mnemosune also combines two things often later distinguished: firstly, what we might now in general terms think of as the human faculty of memory, which stores and restores the past and so structures categories of perception and thought – "holding all things together in the mind and soul" – as the poem has it; and secondly, she generates the Muses, whom we might more usually associate with Imagination. The mythic image of Mnemosune asks us to consider this relationship.

As we have seen, Aeschylus brings this same range of rulership to life in his image of Prometheus, whose name means 'Foresight' (and whose brother was Epimetheus, 'Hindsight'). By stealing fire from the gods and bringing consciousness to humanity, for which he was punished by Zeus, Prometheus becomes himself an incarnation of human consciousness, giving it voice while suffering its wound. In Prometheus Bound, Aeschylus has him refer to "the Mistress of the Arts and Mother of the Muses," and in one way it makes sense that, in an oral tradition which recited long epic poems in the days before writing, goddesses of the Arts were the daughters of Memory. But the etymology points us still farther back into the mists of a lunar culture before the patriarchal Aryans – whose chief god was Zeus – arrived in around 800 BC, and added their voice to the native myths, changing the old priorities to the new point of view. In Greek myth there is always an older story lurking beneath the official myths, close to the soil and the rhythms of the Moon and the Seasons, often only visible through its underlying images and etymology and rites.

Mnemosune's name derives from *Mene*, 'Moon' and *mosune*, 'wooden house' or 'tower' – so literally means 'the House of the Moon.' As Plato somewhat disparagingly said, the Moon can teach even the very slowest creature to count, and practically all the words in Greek concerned with measurement and mind, menstruation, wisdom and mania, have the Moon root of *Me, Men* or *Ma* in them from the Sanskrit. (*Mene*, Moon; *Mneme*, remembrance; *mnesthenai*, remember, *anamnesis*, recollection; *metis*, wisdom, *mania*, mania, *amnesis*, forgetfulness, etc). In the *Aitareya Upanishad*, for instance, when the heavenly bodies are asked to find an abode within the human being, we are told that "the Sun became sight and entered the eyes, and the Moon became mind and entered the heart."

Further, the symbolism of the Moon contains without contradiction the ideas of visible change and invisible perpetuity: both the ever-moving phases and the changeless cycle of the whole – for the numbering of days was always resolved into the 'eternal return' of the New Moon, which, for Plato, was the closest thing we have to eternity. This ceaseless drama also requires the ability to think abstractly, holding in the mind the memory of the whole cycle to interpret any one of its visible phases. And in its image of the eternal, the Moon, especially the Full Moon, has always been a Muse, an inspiration leading us beyond the boundaries of time.

I want to suggest that a study of Mnemosune offers us a chance to think about the relation between Memory and Imagination, in the way that we generally and loosely use these two terms. We can see that, in these Greek myths, Memory and Imagination are much more closely allied than they have become so many generations later, if not at times almost indistinguishable. And yet, as Jung reminds us, only fifty generations separate us from the ancient Greeks. I don't want to try and define these ideas in advance of their stories, and end up trapped in a definition that prevents us thinking through the images, so let's explore the ideas as they emerge – through the thoughts of those who made Memory a goddess and gave her children relationships of their own, most of which have endured for two thousand years.

There are four creation myths in ancient Greece: the native Pelasgian, the Homeric, the Orphic and the Olympian. Mnemosune belongs to the Olympian version of creation, first articulated by Hesiod in 700 BC. In Hesiod's *Theogony*, Gaia, (Earth) was the first to arise from Chaos, and she gave birth to Ouranos, (Heaven) and Pontus, (Sea). In the widespread tradition of son-lovers of the goddess, Ouranos became her consort, and together they gave birth to a generation of divinities called the Titans: six goddesses and six gods, among whom were Rhea (the Flowing One), Kronos (Time), Themis (Law), and Mnemosune, Memory. This tells us that the idea of Memory, along with Time and Lawfulness, belongs to the structure of consciousness – the archetypal realm of the psyche – such that consciousness cannot be conceived without it.

In the next stage of this creation myth, Rhea and Kronos give birth to three daughters - Hestia (goddess of the Hearth), Demeter (goddess of the Harvest), and Hera (whose name means Sacred), and then three sons, Poseidon (god of the Sea), Hades (god of the Underworld) and lastly Zeus, whose name, from its Indo-European roots, means 'Light' and 'Day' or rather, in its original verbal form, the moment of 'Lighting up.' ('Theos,' God, was said in the moment of revelation). Zeus then unites with the goddesses of the older order, the Titans, the nymphs, and the indigenous Pelasgian goddesses of Earth and Moon, bringing the history and native laws of the land into the new order.

Formally married to his sister, cow-eyed Hera, Zeus unites with two of the Titan daughters of Earth and Heaven – firstly with Themis, Law, who brings forth the Horai, the Seasons, and the Moirai, the Fates: and then with Mnemosune, who gives birth to the Muses. The story went that Zeus and Mnemosune lay together for nine nights, and, later, on snowy Olympos she delivered nine daughters, one for each night, all with the same nature, their one thought singing and dancing, and their hearts free from care. They live beside Himeros (Desire) and the Three Graces. From their shrine in their dancing grounds – the *Museion*, from which our term 'museum' comes – they go back and forth in procession to Olympos, wrapped in veils of white mist.

When the Muses sang – about the immortal gods, their ways and laws – "telling of things that are, that will be and that were" (*Hesiod*, lines 41-2) everything stood still: sky, stars, sea and rivers, and, conversely, the mountain that does not move, Mount Helicon, began to grow in rapture up to heaven, until the winged horse Pegasus struck the mountain with his hooves, and the cascade of water arising from the blow was called *hippou krene*, the 'fountain of the horse.' Here is an image of ecstasy beyond the bounds of time and space, when, in playful paradox, Imagination (Pegasus, who came into being soaring from the severed head of the Gorgon of Fear) itself creates reality, bringing the mountain down to earth. Around this spring the Muses danced, and its waters brought inspiration to all who drank from it.

The Muses, who were called not just Mousai but Mneiai, a plural of Mnemosune, could assume the shape of birds, messengers of the unknown, and were also seen as mountain and fountain nymphs, just as their mother was always linked with water, the mysterious source of springs and rivers in the outer and inner worlds, above and below. "It is because of the Muses and the archer Apollo that there exist on earth people who sing songs and play the lyre; kings come from Zeus." The *Hymn to the Muses and Apollo* continues: "If the Muses love you then you are blessed and sweet sound flows from your mouth." The *Orphic Hymn to the Muses* says to them:

> You give birth to virtue in every discipline,
> you nourish the soul and set thought right
> you taught the sacred and mystic rites to mortals.

We have to imagine seeing these Muses outside, embodied in Nature, as well as those who come into our minds in solitude. They come from a time when divinity was immanent in natural life, so they were seen dancing in the waters when they sparkled, and when the mountains shimmered in the evening light, they had come to play. Numinosity was the sign of their presence (literally, 'the nod or wink of a god,' the awakening of the divine). Our term 'musing' may have gained overly inward overtones, but there is also music.

In Boeotia, Hesiod's own country, the Muses were said to be originally only three in number, and had names which come from the craft of poetry: Melete, (Practice) Mneme, (Memory) and Aoide, (Song). But, for Hesiod himself, there were nine Muses and he gives them names eloquent of their natures. These are visions of delight and pleasure, images of beauty that inspire us beyond our daily selves, even our entirely conscious selves. They point to the dimension in any creative work, which is not chosen but 'given' – it comes upon us and takes us away – and for the Greeks 'given' meant 'divinely given' or, as we might say, archetypally infused.

In Book Two of the *Iliad*, the poet asks the Muses to tell him who went to fight in the Trojan War: "For you are goddesses, watching all things, knowing all things, but we have only hearsay and not knowledge." And he ends with the plea that it is the Muses who have to remember it, and give him their memories of it, because he could not do this by himself. When the Muses, as daughters of Mnemosune, are themselves asked to *remember* the past, they are asked to bring back not just the facts but the original structure of feeling in which these facts made sense and had value, which makes them now worth the remembering. The original value, implicitly evoked by the beauty of the Muses who graced the poet with their presence, is thereby transferred to the theme and manner of his song so that it becomes poetry.

The gift of the Muses was then the power of true speech, and the poet was known as the servant or messenger of the Muses, dependent, ultimately, on 'the Muse' for inspiration, as poets have said ever since. So poet and seer, the oracular voice, are allied here, as they are, etymologically, in many Indo-European languages. Both reveal hidden truth, and even, for Virgil in the *Georgics*, the secrets of nature. But there is a warning: the Muses tell Hesiod they can also lie. In fact they seem to tempt him with lies first; the truth, the reservations of the prose imply, is more difficult. As they say: "We know enough to make up lies which are convincing, but we also have the skill, when we've a mind, to speak the truth." So is this mind of theirs arbitrary and unpredictable, or can it be intuited and anticipated? The stories suggest that it is *our* relation to the Muses which calls forth from them truth or trickery.

The nine daughters of the Macedonian king Pierus once challenged the Muses to a contest, with the nymphs as judges. When the Muses won, they punished the girls for their presumption by turning them into chattering magpies. When the Sirens (the half-bird maidens against whose irresistible song Odysseus strapped himself to the mast of his ship) competed with the Muses and naturally lost, the Muses plucked out the Sirens' feathers to make themselves crowns. The Muses were judges in the contest between Marsyas and Apollo for mastery of the flute. Marsyas, the beautiful human flute player, had boasted that he was better than the god. When they judged Marsyas the loser, he was flayed alive.

Approaching the Muses, as any other god or goddess, with hubris – the arrogance of the ego – turns their powers against us. So it is that Homer, Virgil, Dante and even Milton respectfully begin their poetry by invoking 'the goddess,' who may be Mnemosune herself, or the Muses, her daughters. Yet this radical uncertainty – Is the mind pure enough? How can we know? – pervades many tales. The bee maidens, whom Apollo gave to Hermes, teach divination and speak the truth graciously after they have fed on golden honey. "But if they are deprived of the sweet food of the gods they tell you lies, swarming to and fro." How can we tell if they have had their honey? Perhaps by their swarming, their not being in the mood? So that's when not to ask them. Likewise Apollo expects humans to know their place. Some human beings, he says, "shall profit from my oracular voice. Those who come guided by the cry and the flights of prophetic birds, but those who trust in twittering birds and want to question my oracles against my will, in order to know more than the ever-living gods, these people will come on a wasted journey." And even Hermes: "A few he helps, but he endlessly beguiles the race of human beings in the darkness of the night." (*Homeric Hymn to Hermes*). Similarly with dreams: do they come from the Gate of Horn or the Gate of Ivory, the one true and the other deceitful?

Perhaps the tales themselves suggest to us the way of right approach? For while the poet asks the Muses to remember for him so he can repeat it, the first gift of the Muses to the poet, in direct inversion, is forgetfulness – Lethe or Lesmoysne. Lesmoysne is the sister of Mnemosune, suggesting how inextricably the two ideas are linked and valued. When the Muses, or their bard, sing:

> At once that man forgets his heavy heart,
> And has no memory of any grief,
> So quick the Muses' gift diverts his mind.
>
> (Hesiod, *Theogony*, 105-8)

The same word for 'forgetfulness' is used here as in the Orphic Hymn *Lethe*, and while there, for the initiates, it was to be shunned, here, for the poets, it is to be welcomed. So as well as more than one meaning to Memory we have, predictably enough, more than one meaning to forgetfulness. We might read the Muses' gift of forgetfulness as diverting and even redirecting the troubled conscious mind afflicted by its own personal memories which keep it focused on itself alone. So here we are enabled to forget ourselves in order to become open to something larger than ourselves, which the myth describes as a remembering of our origins.

All the stories explore this relation, almost a dance, between forgetting and remembering, with the two terms expanding in meaning until they invoke the whole person, our unconscious as well as our conscious selves. It is the context that gives them their value in each case, the particular story of the psyche which they are imagined to explore. We might even wonder if, between them, it is Remembering and Forgetting, in their daily dance, which creates the underlying reality of the present for each person?

Can we not feel an archetypal forcefield at work in the realm of the mythic Imagination? Stories and images echo each other, cross over and tangle and disentangle, all the while following an invisible thread that winds its way through them all. It is like a mind exploring ever new ways of trying to get at an essence which in the end always escapes us, must escape us, because it can only be glimpsed indirectly through its symbols, which never completely reveal their meaning. The depths of a symbol remain in the Unconscious or they wouldn't involve and compel us as symbols: they would be allegories, optional alternatives, and we could describe them rationally by referring them to something else, or by restating them in a different way.

I have tried to suggest that we cannot simply 'remember' archetypal images in the way we remember a personal event in our past. We can approach them only as symbols for which we need Imagination. They may seem like memories because of the feeling that we have encountered them before, or know them deep within ourselves, and also perhaps because of the intense effort required to bring them back into consciousness – like Orpheus bringing Eurydice back up out of the underworld. (If we look too soon, with 'single' not 'double' vision, as Blake says, we lose them). Whatever we manage to retrieve creates a new whole – the literal meaning of *re*, 'again,' and *member*, a 'piece' – to piece together again, to make into one complete 'body,' like the re-membering of Osiris, Dionysos and Orpheus. True 'Remembrance' requires Imagination and Memory working together as one.

In Yeats' terms this is a joining of the personal memory to the Great Memory. Our little memories, he says, "are but a part of some Great Memory that renews the world and men's thoughts age after age, and ...our thoughts are not, as we suppose, the deep, but a little foam upon the deep." In his *Essay on Magic* he writes that "Whatever the passions of man have gathered about, becomes a symbol in the Great Memory," which, he explains, is the "Memory of Nature herself." Elsewhere, he calls the Great Memory the 'Great Mind', and the *Spiritus Mundi* or *Anima Mundi*, the Soul of the World. This is memory not only in the sense of remembrance of things past but rather as the original pattern holding all the forms that have been and are yet to come. Like the Collective Unconscious, Yeats' World Soul or Great Memory is not set apart from us, for our own memories and dreams are a part of it as It is of us, all indissolubly entwined and so continually, if imperceptibly, changing. We reach it through our passions, some 'mysterious tide in the depths of our being' – and then again we invoke it by engaging with such symbols through Imagination, for this Memory is, as he says, "still the Mother of the Muses, though men no longer believe in it." And is not "Imagination ...always seeking to remake the world according to the impulses and the patterns in that Great Mind, and that Great Memory?"

DIARY OF A WIND POEM

ALICE OSWALD

Dear John

I'VE ALWAYS LOVED the brackets in your letters (as if your voice was continually being undermined by too much thinking,) so here is a poem set in the context of its thinking. I've copied out a few pages from my notebook to offer you some of the dialogue between a poem's final and unfinished voices. Of course there are other voices – fainter and even less finished – that never got as far as the notebook. Imagine them (please) whispering up through every pause and the last voice of all (as in any poem) is Time's, which is why I've structured the notes as a diary …

DIARY OF A WIND POEM

Day 1. Commissioned to write a wind poem, I went down to Bow Creek and made a few notes not looking at the page. I wrote: Unknown. Aside. Convulsive. Compulsive. Unspoken brush-strokes. Critics of stillness. Curse of pure vowels. The cool of the morning. The earth's uncommon sense. When the wind blows, something is affirmed and denied, saying light and dark by turns. Green becomes greener, light is more alive, water understands itself…

This is a dreadful project.

I'm basically asking my breath to describe itself.

How do other people start their poems?

How would the wind write a wind poem?

Describe the wind,

Wind!

Say something marked by discomfort
That wanders many cities and harbours,
Not knowing the language.
Be much-travelled.   *(My notebook is rain-smashed and has no covers.*

It keeps me

Start with nothing but the hair blown sideways   *up to date with myself but I'll*
And say: Gentle   *throw it away when it's finished …)*

South-easterly

Drift

With Rain.   *How should you address the wind?*

Say: Downdraught.   *Twitcher!*

Loiterer!

Anathema!

Big Mouth!

Homer says: "Tell me, Muse, about that much-travelled man …" I like this. I'll steal it. The opening line summons the poem's ending. The poem invokes itself. It's like fetching wood for a fire and by the time it's laid you're too hot.

Day 2. Horrible stifling stillness of a foggy morning. I took the boys down early to their bus and the river had forgotten to retract its ghost. There were a couple of feet of whiteness everywhere as if the trees were only half-made. Reminds me of the bust of an emperor with his lower limbs trapped in a pedestal - just what it's like when a poem is only half-formed …

Come on now Wind, Unglue my fog! I'm waiting!
I keep noticing that rustling noise, an S.O.S. from the trees.

Unglue the fog from the woods from the waist up
And speak disparagingly of leaves.
Be an old man blowing a shell.
Blow over the glumness of a girl   *(I've been reading Lyall Watson's* Glossary of Winds:
Looking up at the air in her red hood   *Aajej, Abrololos, Afer, Alize, Alm, Altanus, Anabatic,*
And say: Suddenly   *Anti-trade, Apeliotes, Aquilo etc as far as Zephyr,*
                Violent   *Zephyrus, Zonda – the hot dry westerly Fall wind…)*
                        Short-lived
                Gust.

Then come down glittering
With a pair of ducks to a rooftop.

I remember standing in a courtyard in my red anorak (I was four at the time) looking glumly at the sky and noticing that the clouds were moving. It terrified me, because I thought the sky was meant to keep steady like a roof. I think this was also when I was first aware of the wind's voice in my hood, very lonely and incoherent.

Day 3. Wrote an email to Kevin Mount, saying I'm stuck in a wind poem and he sent a link to:
OBSERVATIONS OF THE TEMPERATURE OF THE AIR AT SHIGATZE, OR DIGARCHA,
A LARGE TOWN IN GREAT TIBET, 11,800 FEET ABOVE THE SEA

DATE:	HOUR:	NO. THERMOMETER	THERMOMETER	REMARKS	
1865					
Nov. 14	1	...	41.50	Very slight wind from SW	Clear sky
Nov. 14	2	...	43.25	Wind lulled	Ditto
Nov. 14	3	...	44.25	Slight wind from W	Ditto
				Ditto	Ditto
				Ditto	Ditto
				Ditto	Ditto
				Ditto	Ditto
				Strong wind from W	Ditto
				Ditto	Ditto
				Slight W wind	Ditto
				Ditto SE	Ditto
				Ditto SE	Ditto
				Ditto S	Ditto
				Ditto E	Ditto
				Ditto W	Ditto
				Ditto N	Ditto
				Very slight wind from NE	Ditto
				Ditto	Ditto
				Ditto	Ditto
				Ditto	Ditto
				Ditto	Ditto
				Wind lulled	Ditto
				Ditto	Ditto
				Ditto	Ditto
				Ditto	Ditto
				Ditto	Ditto

Go on. Be North-easterly.
Be enough chill to ripple a pool.
Be a rumour of Winter.
Whip the green cloth off the hills
And keep on quietly
Lifting the skirts of women not wanting to be startled
And pushing the clouds like towers of clean linen
Till you get to the Thin
>> **Cry**
>> **That**
>> **Suffers**
>> **On seas.**

Ignore it.

Say: Snow.

Say Ditto.

Those startled women – I've often seen them at Dawlish
Or Aldeburgh, mortified to be reminded of their legs ...

Day 4, which is 5 days later. The body plodding on with its jobs, the mind stockstill in the pause between verse 3 and 4. One day I'll perform a poem in real time, leaving five days between verses. 'Song is after all re-structured time' (Brodsky) and: 'time has its seat within a poem and it is a caesura'.

Wait for five days
In which everything fades except aging.

> *(Foot-tapping... throat clearing... in this struggle between words and something else,*
> *it's only good manners at the end of a line for the poet to defer to her opponent... i.e.*
> *Time. Prose would never have the patience...)*

Then try to describe being followed by heavy rain.
Describe voices and silverings,
Say: Strong
**   Wet**
**   Southwester**
From December to March.

I'll tell you what it's like being followed by heavy rain. Last summer I slept in a rainstorm in my waterproof sleeping bag, too stubborn to give up even when the water was soaking down as far as what felt like my heart. It says in my notebook; 'slept out in the rain. Lovely on my face. I felt like the ground: grateful, I felt like being dead under a tree, water ran sideways between my lips into my ear using me as a leat or gutter. The light rain let me feel like a leaf, the heavy rain forced me to be soil. Weeds could so easily have grown in me. The sky's blackness infact contained mostly mauve and dots of inward light. The wind spoke sometimes in pencil, sometimes in ink. Why do water birds cry out in pain, land birds in joy? I woke as never before, pillowed in birdsong, mainly pigeons.'

Day 5. If you approach the wind with patience then you can strike up some kind of a relationship, as you would with a dog. Certainly something is being more obedient today. There are words like 'leaning' and 'rustling' in the house, instead of 'discomfort' and 'disparagingly'. Is it because of my dream?

(In my dream I bathed in a stone pool, shaped and stepped like a salt crystal. It was dark, it felt supernatural. First slipping down, then loss of mass, then nothing, only sunkness. There were watchers on the edge and one child swam with me but not the other. All this was in a far-off place (perhaps a madness) and that one child was well for ever after, but I could never help the other...)

Describe everything leaning.
Bring a tray of cool air to the back door.   *(But I was always very bored by my*
Speak increasingly rustlingly.   *grandmother telling me her dreams – like*
Say something winged   *looking at someone's holiday snaps.)*
On the branch of the heart.
Say: Song.
Because you know these things.
You are both Breath
    And Breath   *Enter at last the Wind,*
And your mouth mentions me   *an apparition,*
Just at the point where I end.   *carrying its own description ...*

VISITATIONS

Seamus Heaney

THE HISTORY OF poetry contains many accounts of what might be called poetic recognition scenes, meetings where the poet comes face to face with something or someone in the outer world recognised as vital to the poet's inner creative life, and accounts of these meetings represent some of the highest achievements in the art. When a practitioner describes an encounter with a living or dead master, or an equivalent moment of epiphany, something fundamental is usually at stake, often having to do with poetic vocation itself. At the level of autobiography, such scenes record crucial events in the growth or reorientation of the poet's mind; at the mythic level, on the other hand, they can be read as evidence of a close encounter between the poet and the Muse.

What I want to talk about are moments when poets are reminded that theirs is a solemn calling and are made newly conscious of the powers they serve. And that is why I make mention at the very beginning of 'the muse'. Poets in the 21st century are unlikely to invoke her the way Homer invoked her: probably the last one to call upon her in any serious way was John Milton, for although by then the invocation had become thoroughly conventional, in Milton's case the convention was animated and in effect sanctified by his identification of the muse with the Holy Spirit of his three person Christian God. And yet, in spite of the archaic nature of the Muse phenomenon, the several encounters I'll be discussing between the poet and the other still flicker with gleams of mythic light – a light which emanates from an original source in the opening lines of Hesiod's *Theogony*.

Hesiod's dates are as uncertain as Homer's (probably some time in the late 8th or early 7th century BC) although there is firm enough evidence that he was a farmer from the countryside in Boeotia, a man whose life was changed when the Muses, the daughters of memory, appeared at the head of his field and called him to a new task - which task would in turn confer upon him a new authority. A recent prose translation gives Hesiod's account of how he was chosen from among the other 'field-dwelling shepherds' on Mount Helicon, those 'mere bellies' unworthy of the laurel and the gift of inspiration:

> Let us begin to sing from the Heliconian Muses, who possess the great and holy mountain of Helicon and dance on their soft feet around the violet-dark fountain and the altar of Cronus' mighty son...
> One time they taught Hesiod beautiful song while he was pasturing lambs under holy Helicon...And they plucked a staff, a branch of luxuriant laurel, a marvel, and gave it to me, and they breathed a divine voice into me, so that I might glorify what will be and what was before, and they commanded me to sing of the blessed ones who always are, but always to sing of themselves first and last.

So, with Hesiod's foundational story in mind, let me repeat what I said at the start: poetic recognition scenes can be read at the biographical level as significant moments in the growth or reorientation of the poet's mind; while at the mythic level, they can be read as moments of close encounter between the poet and the Muse. And yet these moments of realisation do not always or necessarily involve a face-to-face encounter with some great poetic forebear. In the modern era, the sense of visitation and rededication will often derive from meetings and occasions which are far less exalted, but which are nevertheless bathed in an uncanny light, occasions when the poet has been, as it were, unhomed, has experienced the *unheimlich*.

Even in the modern period, however, the poet typically comes away from such encounters with a renewed sense of election, surer in his or her vocation. What is being enacted or recalled is usually an experience of confirmation, of the spirit coming into its own, a door being opened or a path being entered upon. Usually also the experience is unexpected and out of the ordinary, in spite of the fact that it occurs in the normal course of events, in the everyday world. A strange thing happens. A spot of time becomes a spot of the timeless, becomes, in effect, one of "the hiding places of [the poet's] power."

In the first canto of *The Divine Comedy*, for example, when Dante meets the shade of Virgil, he is not immediately aware that heaven has intervened to send the Latin poet to be his guide, yet a high sense of mystery and destiny does nevertheless prevail; and when, in *Little Gidding*, T. S. Eliot meets a familiar ghost in the dawn light after an air raid in wartime London – a ghost whom Eliot thought of as an emanation of the recently dead William Butler Yeats – there is a similar feeling of mystery and destiny in surroundings that are entirely matter of fact. In both cases, the sense of rare occasion is present in the way the language goes a little bit beyond its usual operations: Dante meets Virgil '*là dove 'l sol tace*' – "where the sun is silent" and that his appearance '*per lungo silenzio parea fioco*' – "seemed fain through long silence"; and in a passage which directly imitates and pays homage to the art of Dante, Eliot says of the stranger he meets "in the uncertain hour before the morning" that he had the look of

> some dead master
> Whom I had known, forgotten, half recalled

Both one and many; in the brown baked features
The eyes of a familiar compound ghost
Both intimate and unidentifiable.

Dante and Eliot are highly self-conscious artificers, and the contexts in which they situate these encounters are unapologetically literary. Your response to what's happening in each case will be enhanced if you happen to know and have a feel for the history of poets and poetry. Neither of them resorts to the ancient invocation of the Muses, but both signal the elevated nature of their experience by recourse to idioms and allusions drawn from the world of high culture. In each case, we are immediately aware that what is at stake is Vocation with a capital 'V'.

Yet direct literary allusion and the appearance of great literary forebears are not the only ways in which poets situate themselves spiritually and artistically. In the age of Freud there was a far more fluid awareness of the sources of inspiration, a much greater readiness to locate the radiance of the gift in those very areas of the pysche that have been the most repressed. D. H. Lawrence's snake, for example, in the poem of that name, is surely a messenger from the hiding place of his own gift, a gift whose operations, Lawrence believed, were obstructed and deformed by the conventional processes of education and socialisation. The snake emerges from a fissure in the earth-wall and trails his slack body down to the water-trough, drinks from it and is then about to withdraw. At which point, Lawrence tells us, he picked up a clumsy log and threw it at the water-trough with a clatter, scaring the snake so that the "part of him that was left behind convulsed in undignified haste,/Writhed like lightning and was gone." "And immediately," the poet goes on, "I regretted it/...I despised myself and the voices of my accursed human education." Which is to say that he realised instinctively that he had sinned against his gift, broken his covenant with the powers in the hiding place, and – as he says in the last lines of the poem, had "something to expiate,/A pettiness."

It is Lawrence's sixth sense that tells him he has something to expiate, and unless a poet continues to follow this sixth sense, he or she is never going to be entirely sure of the creative ground. And the reason for this is fairly obvious and fairly simple, and was stated with characteristic directness by the late Ted Hughes. A poet's first duty, Hughes wrote, is to his gift, and yet, as he also wrote, "Many considerations assault [the poet's] faith in the finality, wisdom and sufficiency of his gift. Its operation is not only shadowy and indefinable. It is intermittent. It has none of the obvious attachment to publicly exciting and seemingly important affairs... in which his intelligent contemporaries have such confidence and so it receives no immediate encouragement."

And Hughes goes on: "Certain memories, images, sounds, feelings, thoughts, and the relationships between these, have for some reason become luminous at the core of his mind: it is in his attempt to bring them out, without impairment, into a comparatively dark world, that he makes his poems."

For a dedicated poet, in other words, the achievement of a true poem is a way of establishing self-worth in a world that does not necessarily regard poetry as being of any great worth in itself. Let me therefore proceed to consider a poem which had just such a resolving effect on the poet who wrote it, a poem by Wordsworth now known canonically as 'Resolution and Independence', but originally referred to by the poet and his circle as 'The Leech Gatherer'. The incident upon which the poem is based was recorded by the poet's sister in her Grasmere journal.

"We met an old man almost double," Dorothy Wordsworth writes on 3rd October 1800. "He had on a coat thrown over his shoulders... Under this he carried a bundle and had an apron on and a night cap...

His trade was to gather leeches, but now leeches are scarce and he had not the strength for it. He lived by begging and was making his way to Carlisle, where he would buy a few godly books to sell. He said leeches were very scarce partly owing to this dry season, but many years they have been scarce... He had been hurt in driving a cart, his leg broke his body driven over, his skull fractured."

Already in the Wordsworths' time, the occupation of leech gathering was dying out, and the character in William's poem, who is recognisably the one described here by Dorothy, is now facing a drastic economic crisis. But when William comes to write about him, his concern is not primarily with the old man's economic prospects. What absorbs the poet, what awakens his Imagination and his powers of incantation is the equanimity with which the old man faces his crisis:

> Himself he propped, his body, limbs and face,
> Upon a long grey shaft of shaven wood,
> And still as I drew near with gentle pace
> Beside the little pond or moorish flood,
> Motionless as a cloud the old man stood
> That heareth not the loud winds when they call,
> And moveth altogether, if it move at all.

* * *

> He told me that he to this pond had come
> To gather leeches, being old and poor –
> Employment hazardous and wearisome!
> And he had many hardships to endure;
> From pond to pond he roamed, from moor to moor,
> Housing, with God's good help, by choice or chance,
> And in this way he gained an honest maintenance.

The old man still stood talking at my side,
But now his voice to me was like a stream
Scarce heard, nor word from word could I divide;
And the whole body of the man did seem
Like one whom I had met with in a dream,
Or like a man from some far region sent
To give me human strength by apt admonishment.

Here, as in the case of Hesiod, of Dante, of Eliot, of Lawrence, and, one might add, of Elizabeth Bishop who, when she looked through the window of her bus, saw into the big 'othering' eyes of a moose that had come out of the *selva oscura* of the Maine woods – here, as in all those cases, the admonishing agent is one who appears in a haunted, dreamy light, like a messenger "from some far region sent." We experience absorption in an other life: in each case, the poet arrives on the scene either abstracted or disoriented, and is then brought more fully alive to his or her obligations and capacities – is helped, in fact, to get back in touch with his or her proper poetic gifts. The writing has a mesmeric effect, and one senses that the composition of the poem must have had a similar self-mesmerising effect upon the poet: "Certain memories, images, sounds and feelings, and the relationship between these, have [indeed] become... luminous at the core of [each] poet's mind" and the encounter serves to remind him or her of the priority of those memories and images, and the poetic obligation he or she owes to them – the obligation, that is, to bring these personally vital bits of psychic life out "without impairment, into a comparatively dark world."

Much, much more could be said about 'Resolution and Independence' but at this point I want to pass on to a poem of my own which was written more than forty years ago, during the Easter holidays of 1970. It is called 'The Tollund Man' and it could carry as its epigraph Wordsworth's lines, "And the whole body of the man did seem/Like one whom I had met with in a dream." And yet the whole body of the man who inspired my poem had appeared to me only in photographs. In fact, by the time the poem got written, all that remained of the body in question was a head, preserved nowadays in a display case in a small museum at Silkeborg in Jutland, not far from the city of Aarhus. But those photographs had an effect on me comparable to the effect of the leech gatherer on Wordworth. It was as if the Tollund Man and I had come together from far away to a meeting where there was something familiar between us yet something that was also estranging and luminous.

The figure in question had been known to the world in general since the evening in May 1950 when he was dug up out of a bog at Tollund by two old brothers cutting peat for their kitchen range. I first met the Tollund Man, however, in a book published in 1969, a translation of a work by the Danish archaeologist P.V. Glob, entitled in English *The Bog People*, but the effect of the meeting was instantaneous. Opening Glob's book was like opening a gate, crossing a line into a new field where the air was headier, the ground more mysteriously ancestral, the sense of scope altogether more ample. I was entranced first and foremost by the image of the old Dane's head and face, seen in black and white, in almost life-size close-up. The man had been strangled, and around what remained of his neck there was a coil of rope, yet the features were in repose. The look of serenity may have been produced by the pressure of the bog over the course of fifteen or twenty centuries, although there was speculation that the resigned expression came from the fact that the man had been a willing participant in a fertility rite. This, Glob suggested, could have involved his being betrothed to the goddess of the earth, being paraded on a wagon as her bridegroom, and being bedded down with her in the bog – so that spring should return and the cycle of nature be renewed.

For whatever reason, there was indeed a rare composure about the man's demure mouth, his slightly bristled upper lip and the faint glisten of the skin on his closed eyelids. I knew from the scientific evidence that this was the head and face of a northern European countryman of the Iron Age, preserved in the peat for the best part of two millennia, yet he felt as close and familiar to me as my Great Uncle Hughie, who had a similar bristle on his long upper lip and a similar weathered look that suggested both stoicism and a capacity for survival. At the same time, the head had the stillness and focus of a votive object. It did not appear like human remains. It invited contemplation, seemed capable of putting one in touch with the timeless. And yet if it could have spoken, it looked as if it might have said the kind of thing that my old uncle might have said. "Aye, son, times are hard," it might have remarked, "but aren't we hard too?"

By Easter 1970 times were indeed hard in Northern Ireland, and in a prefatory poem in *Wintering Out* (1972) I wrote that we were "hug[ging] our little destiny again," although the poem in the book which really took the measure of the times was 'The Tollund Man.' Although it rehearses different images of death and atrocity committed in the course of twentieth century Irish wars of independence and attrition, the main focus is on the iconic head, a head which had the same kind of brown baked features as Eliot's familiar compound ghost, and which possesses to this day the same look of being "forgotten, half-recalled, both one and many." And just as Eliot fixed what he called "a pointed scrutiny" on the face of his dawn walker, so I gazed with complete entrancement at my familiar ghost, as if he were indeed "a man from some far region sent/To give me human strength by apt admonishment."

This, then, is the poem:

i

Some day I will go to Aarhus
To see his peat-brown head,
The mild pods of his eye-lids,
His pointed skin cap.

In the flat country nearby
Where they dug him out,
His last gruel of winter seeds
Caked in his stomach,

Naked except for
The cap, noose and girdle,
I will stand a long time.
Bridegroom to the goddess,

She tightened her torc on him
And opened her fen,
Those dark juices working
Him to a saint's kept body,

Trove of the turfcutters'
Honeycombed workings.
Now his stained face
Reposes at Aarhus.

ii

I could risk blasphemy,
Consecrate the cauldron bog
Our holy ground, and pray him

To make germinate

The scattered, ambushed
Flesh of labourers,
Stockinged corpses
Laid out in the farmyards,

Tell-tale skin and teeth
Flecking the sleepers
Of four young brothers,
Trailed for miles along the lines.

iii

Something of his sad freedom
As he rode the tumbril
Should come to me, driving,
Saying the names

Tollund, Grauballe, Nebelgard,
Watching the pointing hands
Of country people,
Not knowing their tongue.

Out there in Jutland
In the old mankilling parishes
I will feel lost,
Unhappy and at home.

The minute I wrote the lines, "Some day I will go to Aarhus/To see his peat brown head,/the mild pods of his eyelids,/His pointed skin cap," I found myself in a new field of force. The stanza felt like a vow and this act of poetry a matter of deep import. It was serious speech at a serious time. I was looking at a photograph but was promising to go on what was, in effect, a pilgrimage to the actual head. I had been reoriented, afforded a deeper sense of calling, led to a place in myself that needed discovery, "lost, unhappy and at home."

This is an example of what the writing of a poem can do: it can lead the writer out of himself or herself, provide an experience of estrangement, and then resituate him or her in the usual life, bemused, as it were, as if for a moment the gift for uttering truth had been possessed, as if from a laurel tree luxuriantly in bloom the Muses broke a branch and gave it for a staff and breathed a sacred voice into the mouth. Or to make the case more autobiographically, with reference to 'The Tollund Man': here was a poem written at a time when the literary scene in Northern Ireland was buzzing with debate about how the poets should be responding to the crisis in their society, a time when symposia were sizzling with the contributions of intelligent contemporaries and the ideologues were full of intensity about these exciting public events. And in that confusing Babel, my total immersion in the element of the bog man was a reminder of the necessary extra dimension and the truly credible order of poetry itself.

THE PROJECT

Andrew Miller

IT HAS NO end other than our own. It will not arrive anywhere, will not conclude.

Its posture is that of readiness, of any wild thing in any wild wood, watching, listening.

It makes, at most, a slight humming sound. It makes the sound of slow human breathing.

It is neither male nor female. Neither young nor old.

It brings light. It helps us to think. It offers the (still) underrated consolation of truth.

It is communal, not competitive.

No one will die (immediately) if it stops.

It sharpens our responses.

It insists on plurality.

It haunts all tyrants.

It respects itself, but only enough to defend itself, to go on.

It is practical, tenacious.

It is strong as the bones of a little fish.

It can be shared though not stolen. Buried but not killed.

It has little to do with education. It has much to do with desire.

Systems embrace it but cannot own it. (The vanity of power is frightening and enormously funny.)

It lives on coffee, wine, tobacco. On Sencha tea drunk at midnight. On numerous medicines.

It is lichen on a bare stone wall.

It is the song half-heard, the dripping of gutters, the lovers in the next room.

Those who work for it are not priests or samurai or wire-walkers. They are not prostitutes or rock-climbers or actors or professional cross-dressers. It may be necessary, however, to be all and any of these at a moment's notice.

Those who work for it have no more 'character' than a pea-flower, a nettle.

To work for it nothing more is needed than to be in it "with all your heart."

The work is sometimes beautiful, sometimes dull.

It is a relisher of imperfection.

It is the hammer of insincerity.

It is neither a religion nor a game yet always playful, always full of wonder.

It is Prévert reaching for his matches, Colette laughing in the mirror, Lowell checking-out of the asylum.

It is bare-headed and shod as a pilgrim.

It is heroic.

It is plain as a man's hands.

It does not 'stand' for anything.

And so on. (You continue the list.)

LURED INTO THE LIGHT:
THE VOICE OF THE POET

ADAM THORPE

I HAVE OFTEN tried to work out why, when we read (as opposed to hear) poems, there are two voices. There is our own voice interpreting the printed letters in our head in that alchemical act we call reading, and there is the voice of the poet. Do they interweave in a kind of unsounded canon? Does one take up a certain percentage of the dial, and the other the remainder? Is the poet a kind of auditory tone or pitch, the underlying drone, and the reader the clear soloist? And is there any truth in the assertion that the finer the poem, the easier it is to hear its creator?

What about a poem like *The Waste Land*, a collage of parody and allusion and fragmented myth, of dramatic speech and mystical prayer, of demotic pub-talk and literary pastiche? How on earth can Eliot's voice survive through what was basically a severe scissoring job by Ezra Pound? But it does. There is a secret musculature, a pulse, a unique presence. Think of Shakespeare, the pressure of a singular mind behind a myriad of characters. Think of Yeats, who through all his poetic mutations tunes the stream to the same inimitable murmur. This has nothing to do, of course, with the poet's *actual* out-loud utterance: in scratchy recordings, we hear Yeats put all his verse through the same intoned dirge, claiming that rhythm is all – while simultaneously flattening its liveliness.

Years later, Eliot was to dismiss *The Waste Land* as a "piece of rhythmic grumbling," which says more about it than many a critical tome. It is the record of a social, temporal and personal breakdown, refracted through a single consciousness. It has all the hallmarks of severe depression, that lonely determination to see bleakness in all. "April is the cruellest month," it scowls as an opener, chewing up Chaucer's sweet celebration of the pilgrim's season – and every sap-rising lyric since. We know where we are, at least: this is the twentieth century staggering out of its first great disaster, its broken sentences echoing in a Lausanne sanatorium, the long windows surveying a Europe thick with young men's ghosts. The patient – a bank clerk – is ill, memories come and go unbidden: half-hallucination, half symbolic drama that connects nothing with nothing. The overall effect is majestic, like a shattered temple.

After Eliot's Pound-hacked grumble, romanticism seemed definitively last year's style; most poetry became more narrow-eyed and suspicious, wary of nature-adulation, keener on the urban, checking the Muse's street-cred. It did not do away with the voice, however, that unique human timbre that is, in its own way, a cause for celebration in itself. "Poetry… survives," Auden famously wrote in a poem that begins in the bleakest midwinter midnight of our times, on the eve of the Second World War and on the very ice-locked day that Yeats died: "It survives,/A way of happening, a mouth." A poem is utterance, even if it never leaves the reader's head: spittle-free, no stumbling.

Auden's 'mouth' is not a generalised mouth. Marketing is the latter (think of the smarmy cold call), as is politics, business, the media or, alas, much of publishing. These are huge mouths, so huge you can see the pixels. A poem's mouth is lifesize and unique and its breath is in your ear: it is intimate. It passes things on that, selfishly, you feel are meant only for you. A poem's message cannot be relayed over speakers. You seldom disagree with a poem, as you so often disagree with a statement. You hardly ever detest a poem, either, as you might well detest a prose work (even a novel).

This is maybe because, as John Fowles once put it in a break from being the celebrated novelist he loathed (his first love was poetry): "I never pick up a book of poems without thinking that it will have one advantage over most novels: I shall know the writer better at the end of it."

And what if you know the poet already – as a friend or an acquaintance or (if you are a poet yourself) a fellow dreamer?

Oddly, this makes no difference. The actual everyday voice is washed over by the deeper voice, the voice of the Imagination, or the daimon, or what used to be called the soul. Were we to have known him personally, we would not have heard Keats's Enfield accent in 'Ode to a Nightingale'. And neither do we quite hear our own accent, to come back to my original point.

When I read John Moat's poems, his actual charming and inimitable tones – forever seeming to negotiate what he once called a "thermal of delight" (referring to his grandchildren) – do not interfere. I use the term 'interfere' without meaning to dilute the joy of Moat's presence, whether down the line or in full and lanky person. When I read his verse – which I have done over and over down the years, being an unremitting fan – I hear his heart, not his vocal chords. Not all his heart, I suppose, but a fair bit of it: perhaps even more than he realises[1]. I hear his heart and his place, his subtle-body place and his actual, geographically-honed place – the notched bit of coast-line, the lane, the oaks, the house, the garden, and O blessed spot, the hut. THE hut. And all huts. That's to say, the hut you could never Google-street. With

[1] "Do we ever know how much of ourselves we give away? Or just deny." (Moat: letter to AT, 2004)

the scent of syringa, the tinkle of the brook, or the thud of the owl's wings that I heard, unbelievably, echoing through his wood, behind us, like the beat of deep-down metre. It was so Moat-ish I thought he was pulling my leg.

His heart-voice was there from the beginning, from *6d per Annum* on, the slim volume printed on paper he and Fairfax found on a dump (or so the legend goes):

> In my garden for some days now
> Flits the shadow of my bird
> In the dark beyond the massive leaves
> Of my magnolia tree he
> Cheeps...

There are three possessive 'my's, but they are not noticed at first. The auditory claim of the bird takes over. Some poets' self-obsession is irritating, or you just learn to live with it when you read them. Moat's is intrinsic to his generosity, so it is a delight. This is why, when his poems speak of depression and breakdown, the effect is more devastating – more so even than Plath or Sexton or Lowell. The ice locks around the reader's heart, too. The devastating poems in *Welcombe Overtures* on the stillborn child are stronger for being tugged against 'joy,' against the stream's current. There is actually a lightness in them which is extraordinarily authentic:

> And the midwife's reply. 'Yes dear, I'm afraid she is.' She
> Rang. Someone brought two cups of tea.
> A daughter then. Then those were a woman's hands
> I saw tug at the folds...

That leap into womanhood, announced by the stammer of the twice-chimed 'then', stands in for the surreality of shock. Why these poems are not in every anthology of twentieth-century verse beats me.

The garden, the shadow, the bird, the leaves, the tree, the birdsong: the missing elements are the boom of the nearby sea and the trickling, immortal stream. This is Moat's locale, his geomantic habitation, from where he has never wandered, even when writing on New Zealand's South Island – his mother's birthplace – in that masterly but home-missing travel log, *Practice*. It reminds me of Michael Longley's *Carrigskeewaun*, or Marvell's "green thought in a green shade," or Dylan Thomas's heron-haunted Welsh bay. It is home, with a status that is not just literary or mythic or symbolic, but real.

Real because we see the writer at work in this home; and we see him in startlingly direct close-up shots not just of the hut but of the tools of his trade:

> Beloved, what am I to do? In the night a spider
> Has slung his web between the keys of my typewriter –
> The A, the & and the ?. Then I'll pick up the windfall thread.

These are among my favourite lines of Moat's. On a QWERTY keyboard the thread must have covered most of the machine in a triangular shape. The first letter, the connecting ampersand, the open-ended question. A simulacrum of a life. Birth and death's mystery with a life's '&' in between – it's a pictographic simulacrum of an elegant knot or a path that overlaps itself. And 'windfall' – what a resonant adjective, only becoming a self-sufficient noun when the subject is apples. In the wonderful late sequence 'Winter Solstice,' the poet dreams in midwinter of the "milk-breath of spring" and of "this dancing girl, her hair adaze with apple blossom…" Another thread.

So I would now at this juncture like to clear my throat, tap the microphone and say of this image that it is Imagination, central to the romantic vision that Moat has inherited in both painting and words from Blake, Palmer, Keats, David Jones or Yeats and which forms the essential pulse behind his and John Fairfax's invention of Arvon. But this is to be reductive: Moat's poetry is not a schema, just as Yeats' later poetry escapes its own dependence on his wife's automatic writing (faked to please her husband) and makes of its hamminess something rich and strange.

And there are, in Moat, recurring images that elide into symbols just as resonant as Yeats' falcons or gyres. They diminish the gap between matter and spirit; they serve as stepping stones or proper bridges. On a long-ago trip to Morocco, Moat glimpsed a young shepherdess on the other side of the river; she became a Muse figure, dark-eyed and unknown except as one of the presiding genii of his verse. Morocco is still an intensely romantic country, where the sight of women in brightly-coloured traditional costume washing clothes in a stream, or loading their field's crop onto a donkey, evokes less a reflection (to a poet at least) on rural poverty or Orientalism, as an intensely nostalgic dream of the simpler life, fulfilling one of Yeats' criteria for civilisation: graceful beauty. For Moat, the Arab girl, or at least her glance over the swirling water, became an image of the feminine.

And the male poet's work, whether in words or paint, is dedicated to imbibing the feminine. As he puts it in his recent essay on Arvon, "the creative balance of feminine and masculine [is] at the heart of all meaning." It is the female within the male that he is intent on awakening, in the process of what Jung called 'individuation' – achieving completeness through, in Moat's words in the same essay, "being individually party to the Imagining." Since the Imagining is a vast, collective entity intrinsic to the natural world[2] (there is more than

[2] "The nonbeliever's paradise," as Rebecca Solnit memorably puts it in *Wanderlust, A History of Walking* (London, 2001). In that context, she is referring to a monotheistic belief.

a hint of pantheism in Moat's philosophy), every individual is "essential to its completeness." It was this belief that motivated the joint Fairfax-Moat project to create a 'home' (literally) for the individual Imagination to sense its own 'intentionality' – remarkably, the energies are such that Arvon's compass is still pointing in roughly the right direction.

Back to the typewriter poem from *Overtures*: the serendipitous "windfall thread" then catches on Keats and his famous image of the poet weaving his own airy citadel as a spider does his web, which Moat effortlessly shifts by way of 'joy' to the Gita's prayer-fluttering figtree that, in turn, embraces "your eyes, my poems, our house, our child, our breath." This was written on the first anniversary of his and Antoinette's marriage: an A to a question mark, since none of us can second-guess the future.

In between we have this crucial line: "And utterance is sole earnest of the creator". Pressuring 'earnest' into a noun, and therefore into its less usual meaning of 'token' or 'presage', brilliantly enacts that 'Omega Point'[3] of the original creation as Word, but it also highlights the lonely idea that, without the poem, there is no poet. Typical of Moat's sensual practice is the audible punching of the typewriter itself in 'utterance' – down to the word's visual echo of the slight cup of each fingertip-friendly key.

Utterance: a silence from the distant hut means gestation; a rattling means production. Silences can be lengthy.

> All winter, not one poem.
> Why the hurry?
> The frozen moment was in store.

---

[3] Teilhard de Chardin's term for the point of maximum complexity and consciousness, towards which the universe and its individuals are evolving by dint of the Point already existing in a transcendent form: the French mystic philosopher has, along with Jung, the Zen master Suzuki, Blake and others, been an abiding presence in Moat's achievement.

This, from the superb sequence *Cold Spell*, is followed by a poem relating an incident that crops up more than once in the poetry: Stroller, the pony belonging to the poet's daughter, goes missing in the frozen landscape. The subsequent sighting of its hoof-prints appears to take place both "in meditation" and in the outer world, in that cruel snow-dusted night. This image of creative discovery may be indebted to Ted Hughes' famous "sharp hot stink of fox,"[4] but Moat's version seems subtler, more allusive, more naturally borne.

Cold Spell shuttles expertly between the inner and outer worlds throughout the sequence, which narrates a particularly harsh winter. The properties of the latter – especially the brilliant light and the eerie silence – are heavily personified: "The light is afraid of waking us." Or they are elementally transmuted: "the frozen valley brimmed with clear sunlight." As if, in a completely stilled natural world, light and silence become physically liquefied.

When, therefore, we look at Moat's poetry whole, we recognise the signals, the signs, immensely subtle or glancing as they can be, on what seems to be a half-conscious, dreaming level. In the aforementioned *Welcombe Overtures* and other earlyish poems such as the remarkable 'And the New Moon Is Her Face' – to be reprised later in uncollected pieces like the beautifully relaxed and intimate 'Water Scales' or the atmospheric prose sequence set in France called *Wine Country* – Moat uses a specific method. In a private letter (2006), he explained to me that he was trying in *Overtures* to "create an idiom in which the underlying myth and the current language could meet, and so have the language rediscover its roots." He would "jaw" about this with Fairfax, whose 'Mare Tranquilitatis' represented his friend and golfing partner's own "way of working it." The mixture of supple rhyme and rhythm and the loose-limbed and generous stanzaic structure represented Moat's particular 'way of saying things,' whose unique, alluring timbre we

---

[4] Moat once amusingly reckoned that the trouble with massive Collecteds is that they always fall open to the same page – in Hughes' case, *The Thought-Fox*.

never lose. This remains true even in much tighter, song-like poems such as 'Life Story' (My father died and left/My mother all to me;/I took her at face value/And that left father free), or the Blakean sequence *Deep within the Seed the Dream*, which includes some haunting rhymed elegies skilfully playing with repetition and anaphora:

> Dear God, was that her crying?
> "Be still," she said, "Whatever's born
> Is a newborn way of dying."

The mysterious, haunting sequence *Opus* from the collection *Firewater & the Miraculous Mandarin*, which reads as an exploration of depression (or at least creative dejection), is prefaced by Jung's assertion that the symbols which express the realm of "subtle reality" are both 'real' and 'unreal.' Jung, a strong influence on Moat – and similarly victim of a breakdown – drew his inspiration from the methods of the ancient alchemists and their mix of down-to-earth curiosity (or simple greed, in many cases) and philosophical wonderment.[5]

In *Opus*, the idiomatic timbre survives in the 'real' part of each recurrent symbol: the key to his poetic universe, or rather to his secret garden door, is that his symbology is both particular and general, whether describing a swan or a hearth or a tree. The garden is both a mythic garden and a real one that needs digging: and, as I have noted, time and again we are drawn to the poet's actual presence in it, even in the act of composing. This, perhaps, is a witness to the abiding influence of the Chinese and Japanese poets on his work: their pebble simplicity in collections like the eighth-century *Man'yoshu*, once dropped into the mind, ripple into both inward and outward realms whose only limits are the reader's own.

Similarly, many of Moat's poems prowl tantalisingly on the

---

[5] For a contemporary version, see Marius Kociejowski's extraordinary account of his friend Suleyman the Syrian Sufi, crouching in front of a Kelvin digital temperature controller in Damascus in an attempt to make gold (*The Street Philosopher and the Holy Fool*, London 2004).

spellbound margins of dream: night occupies its proper place, which as Shakespeare implies in *Macbeth* is a "half-world" – half the globe, half the time.

> And the warm night wind on my cheek
> Or your cheek or your hair or your breath

It is at night that the poet is fully awake to the creative unconscious, to admiration of the lover, to the consciousness of breath, to the Imagination that crystallises – sometimes terrifyingly – around the impish exterior sounds from the darkness (no wonder civilisation is so intent on banishing its depths in sodium orange). These and other elements are heated in the poetry to the point where they fuse, and produce a vision that is thankfully other, indefinable and allusive: a good night-vision, perhaps, that sees clearly, like an owl. As he puts it in *Fiesta*, a group of poems honouring the subversive forces of Mexico's nocturnal Dance of the Dead:

> toward morning the dark wore thin
> the spell grew less certain

Moat's voice is rarely drowned by the symbol, or the frequent alchemical, Gnostic or Buddhist references: the idiomatic streak, the actual texture of the real, somehow remains in creative equilibrium with its abstract or generalised counterpart. This is quite clear in the poet's wonderful letters, which share with Keats's a vivid immediacy and down-to-earthness: "Damn," as he interrupted himself in a recent missive, "that was going to be a hell of a good sentence – when the bloke from Porlock phoned: now let me see..."

It is also clear in his early *The Ballad of the Leat*. This, to my mind, is one of the finest poems of the post-war era. I first heard it rather than read it; Moat gave a reading in the now-defunct Newbury Arts Workshop, housed in an old Temperance Hall with 'Beware the Adder that Stings' and suchlike admonitions carved in stone on its façade. As I was scarcely out of my teens and struggling to be a poet myself, I was easy prey to admiration (although the latter state has only expanded in the thirty-odd years since). Moat's professed desire to weave together idiom, symbol and myth is carried out with such ease in *The Ballad of the Leat* that I am tempted to see pure 'gift' in it, rather than great 'talent' – Moat himself being careful to distinguish between the two. Perhaps the title is misleading: the poem is hardly in ballad metre and although rhymed ABBA, it is often in rhymes so skilfully slanted that the scheme is invisible. Local Devon folk (including his farming neighbours) appear as if they were born to it – which they are, in a way: the real hero being the stream that once worked the mill's wheel.

The poet buys up the mill cheap after the previous owner, having revived the water's flow by repairing "the dam, the walls complete, the leat as well," promptly dies. The Doctor's ghost informs him (as it were) that the leat (the trench that carries the water to the mill-wheel) needs clearing again. A tale-within-the-tale tells of a minor disaster when 'Arthur' (one of the poem's dedicatees) mishandled the sluice stone and the water almost broke the cogs and the wheel itself:

> What did old Bailey say? Arthur smiled: 'He didn't bide
> to ask nort, he set to and laced me to the truth of music.'

Effortlessly then, without any romantic pretension, the leat's music is understood to dictate the poet's inner 'truth' or creativity: "when/the leat ran dry, I too – dry as a bone./It was as if the bone had stuck in my throat." He rescues that first inert cliché of a simile with a deepening instead of a diversion, and the outward and the inward dance in tandem. The image is indistinguishable from the thing itself. And so we continue entranced to the inevitable end, when the balladeer hands Antoinette, in apology for a ruined supper, 'the leat' – which, of course, is the poem itself.

This long poem had quite a profound effect on me, because fresh from studying the difficult modernists (it was the end of the 1970s), and being an unapologetic fan of David Jones and Geoffrey Hill, I saw how contemporary poetry could still tap the vein of clarity and narrative without sounding like a pop lyric. It's hellishly difficult to bring off, of course, which is why the small magazines were full of gnomic, dictionary-raiding verse that simply admired its own incomprehensibility. That shuddery term 'Georgian' threatened any attempt to do otherwise. Which is possibly why *The Ballad of the Leat* and the 30 'love poems' of *Welcombe Overtures* – despite being republished together by Dartington Poetry Press in 1987 – were pretty much ignored. Now that Edward Thomas (for one) is so much in fashion, this may change.

Something Moat said in another of his letters, referring as generously as ever to my own verse, might act as a coda. Few poets are so open to the "gift" of the Imagination – or rather, so openly open. This is why he has been able to broadcast his findings (in the agricultural meaning of the term) so far and wide through Arvon, Tandem, the Yarner Trust and the Extension Trust. He regards himself as a conduit, the leat to the Imagination's inexhaustible flow. What he recognises, and what scintillates in his poetry, is that much of the time we must not work at it, but allow it. It does not come garlanded in flowers and singing, but modestly, from an unexpected direction. And so this passage in one of his letters is what I keep remembering when the sluice-stone slips, when dejection starts to dry the channel's bed:

A magic happens… we give ourselves to the
commonplaces of the reverie and then at the end look
up and find ourselves duped into the light.

ON THE HOOF

for John Moat

You promptly sat down
on the rough stones of our garden steps

and began to paint. Effortlessly it seemed,
but I didn't interrupt. I went

inside and made the tea. You made of the ivy-
covered descent with the neighbour's

abandoned concrete wall
a mystic tunnel (ink, pastel, gouache) ending

on a little bright patch that is our pond.
'It's not there,' I said, 'not visible

from there, it's off to the right.'
'I moved it,' you chuckled, with what

you once called your *Beano-grin*;
'I hope you don't mind, but it has to be done,

sometimes.' Now it's framed and at the bottom
of our staircase (the ivy-trunks violet,

the spurge blue), I see what you mean:
Moat-moved, gleaming by its dark

brush-trail of mint, the pond
is omega at the tunnel's end.

SIXTEENS

LAWRENCE SAIL

I

THERE ARE, of course, no formulæ for the Imagination; nor is it possible to list the conditions in which it will necessarily flourish. On the other hand, it is perfectly possible to describe conditions inimical to its thriving, either personal or social, for instance: acute pain; a society predicated on busyness; an education system with no built-in pauses; clamour of any kind. In this sense its readiest definitions are negative. But at what point, and how, might these be transformed – the howl of pain become a song of lamentation, or an understanding of seething activity and noise heighten a creative awareness of their opposites?

* * *

In truth the Imagination is not anarchic but, rather, anachronistic: not against order (though its imperatives are likely to diverge fundamentally from those of politicians and artocrats,) but against time. The confinement it really challenges is that of mortality.

* * *

The ultimate negativity: can you imagine a world without the Imagination?

* * *

Precisely what makes the Imagination so exhilarating is its inherent combination of paradigm and instance, potential and enactment. What other entity combines these qualities of unchanging substance and limitless variation, of innocence and usage, the universal and the individual?

* * *

Another joy of the Imagination is the way in which it brings together discovery and recognition.

* * *

If a hologram is cut or broken into any number of pieces, each fragment – while still individual in its own shape – retains an image of the whole, even if in lower resolution. This strikes me as an apt emblem for the relation between the Imagination and its individual manifestations.

* * *

In the 1950s there was a hot-rod American evangelical preacher (operating, I think, under the name Colonel Samson, a kind of *nom de doom*) who toured a number of British schools. One of the two sermons he offered began, unforgettably: "If I had a million dollars, I would build a mighty monument a hundred miles long and a hundred miles wide and a hundred miles high, and I would call it 'the Mighty Failure.'" More recently we have had the Millennium Dome, a fine instance of putting the cart before the horse. In the realm of the Imagination, there can be similar temptations – not least the desire to have a Career as a Writer or Poet.

* * *

There are times when the Imagination promotes a creative ability to keep the eye off the ball. For the poet, sometimes, this can take the form of the shadow poem that emerges, paradoxically, as a bonus of intense concentration on another poem: the poem in hand joined by at least one from the bush.

* * *

Insofar as the Imagination has to do with community and communication, you'd think the present time would be an advantageous one. It's an irony that the age of broadband can be so narrowing, and to find that globalisation has fragmentation as its corollary. It's hard to talk of this without appearing luddite, and of course new generations will find their own idioms and emphases and know, more than their elders might give them credit for, what weight and worth to give to new technologies. These may be indeed simply beyond the Imagination of those brought up with carbon paper and the use of a razor blade to correct typing errors. Yet, whatever adaptive virtues and skills may emerge, it's also hard not be concerned about some of the consequences, actual and potential, of our new systems. Some of these centre on the simple matter of speed: the risks of approximation, superficiality, a lack of giving proper consideration.

* * *

One definition of teaching in schools: smuggling the Imagination through.

* * *

The Imagination delights in mirrors and games, and can accommodate easily what we only imagine we imagine.

* * *

At the frontiers of utilitarian relevance, perhaps the Imagination has nothing to declare. Yet hasn't it often been a leap of the Imagination that has enabled the crossing of the threshold to discoveries, some with important practical implications?

* * *

Paying attention, a form of slowing down, is often a threshold to the Imagination, as can be also, for children, the experience of boredom. For adults, on a car journey it's good to be able to view a breakdown as an invitation to study the verges usually raced past in a blur.
Sometimes the workings of the Imagination are curtailed by being committed too soon to paper or screen. As a culture we have recourse to the written word very readily: it's interesting to see what may happen when, instead of reaching for the notebook as soon as an image or an idea occurs, we harbour and hatch.

* * *

Those who disbelieve the environmental consequences of human exploitation and pollution may be suffering not only from denial, but a failure of the Imagination, whose logic would tell them that one possible outcome of a consumer society is a cannibal society.

* * *

I once invited a student to tell me the tense of a verb in a French text we were reading. He thought for some time, in the way people do when they haven't a clue but feel they should give an impression of deep contemplation and effort, goodwill standing in for knowledge. Finally he ventured, "Is it the operatic present?" Perhaps the proper tense for the workings of the Imagination would be 'the infinite present.'

* * *

II

THE QUICK

for John

Not just a kiss –
the unthinking heart,
or a wound tender
in all its hurt,
not just those children
laughing in the leaves,
or the radial blur
of fields seen
from a speeding train,
but like a bird
cherished, in hands
cupped as if
for prayer, and the mind
taking on the tempo
of all that lasts,
all that is gone.

ADVENTURES IN THE UNDERWORLD

Lindsay Clarke

LIKE THAT OF many other novelists, my storyteller's Imagination was first fired by a childhood encounter with the folktales told for centuries by the people of Europe. Unsigned, free from all claims of ownership, the birthright property of everyone, they have been passed on from one generation to the next until they grew smooth as pebbles in the passing. Some of their features may even have sprung from those early ancestral moments when people first began to shape their experience of the world by telling stories; but, whatever the case, their elemental magic can still illuminate and enchant our lives today. For that reason, the colours, feel and smell of the copy of *Grimm's Fairy Tales* which my mother bought for me from Woolworth's remain alive to my senses nearly seventy years later.

I clearly remember the way story after story opened on a bright, heraldic realm that was far removed from the industrial landscape of northern England where I was growing up, yet evidently accessible within it. One simply opened the door of the book and passed through into a dream-like terrain where improbable and contradictory things seemed to happen with such fluency that one happily took them for granted. It felt as though they were obeying laws of nature different from, but as powerful in their way as those that prevailed in the world outside. And though fashions have changed and those old stories no longer figure in children's bedtime reading as strongly as they once did, isn't it possible that they have survived for so many centuries precisely because they offer to each new generation life-quickening images of the way those laws can work for us?

Consider, for instance, the story of The Three Feathers, a tale which feels apposite here because a quill feather was for many centuries the standard writing implement. The story tells how a sick and ageing king was uncertain which of his three sons should be his heir, so he set them to compete on three separate quests, dropping feathers to see which direction each should take. On the first quest they were sent to bring home the finest carpet. The eldest son followed the feather that blew to the east, the second son chased his feather westwards, while the third and youngest son – the simpleton – watched his feather merely fall to the ground at his feet. Looking down, he saw a previously unnoticed trap-door there, opened it, lowered himself into the empty space, and climbed down a shaft deep into the earth where he came upon a wise toad that gifted him with what proved to be the most splendid carpet of the three. To his brothers' disgust he emerged as the winner of the second quest too when the toad presented him with a priceless ring. The last prize to be gained was a future queen, and the simpleton rewarded the toad for all its help by choosing the creature for his bride. On their return to the surface, his loyalty of heart was rewarded in turn when he saw the toad transform into the most beautiful young woman anyone had ever seen. Needless to say, he won the kingdom as well as a good wife.

If you have been educated into the literalistic conviction that such things are impossible in a world where tadpoles may turn into toads but on no account are toads allowed to turn into princesses, then you may dismiss this tale at first glance as a childish piece of hokum. But small children don't have that problem – not, that is, until adults put it in their way; nor do they judge such stories at first glance. They listen to them again and again, and their delight often visibly increases at each repetition. Given that stricter minds than mine have serious reservations about some features of these tales, why should this be?

I think it's because children intuitively understand that such stories nourish their powers of Imagination just as surely as their bones are strengthened by milk. What's more, the pleasure that such stories give them may have less to do with the fascination of strangeness than with the surprise of recognition. For yes, the story I've just told is about a king and his sons, the feathers and a talking toad; but isn't it also about our talent for bringing something new to life through the mysterious processes of self-discovery? And if so, doesn't it offer important truths about the nature and laws of the Imagination? For when things seem insolubly stuck or in decay (that is, in the idiom of the story, when the king is sick), then for renewal to happen, change will be required, and change is what the active power of the Imagination (otherwise known as magic) is all about. Often enough, as the story illustrates, such change is accomplished not by casting about on the surface of things but by risking a descent into the dark places of the underworld where the seeds of new life lie. And to make such a journey successfully we must rely on what is youngest inside us – our primal innocence with its willingness to be thought simple or stupid in its loyalty to unworldly values – but also on what is oldest, the wise, serpentine power of the instincts which have their origin deep in the unifying intelligence of the earth itself. For toads, as Shakespeare reminds us in *As You Like It*, can sometimes have precious jewels in their heads.

Such tales about transforming journeys to the underworld are found worldwide in folktales, myths and what we have been taught to call 'high art.' A very ancient Sumerian poem tells of the descent of Inanna into an underworld where the laws are "perfect and not to be questioned." Famously, Book XI of Homer's great poem *The Odyssey* tells how the hero entered Hades to consult the shades of the dead. In Virgil's *Aeneid* the hero descends into Hades where he is granted a prophetic vision of Rome's future; while in the first part of his *Divine Comedy*, Dante is led by Virgil into the underworld of the Inferno and is there shown a Christian vision of the torments of Hell. More recent fictional accounts, though not immediately recognisable as underworld experiences, follow a similar katabatic pattern. Among their other complexities, what else are Marlow's voyage into the *Heart of Darkness*, Hermann Hesse's *Journey to the East*, Doris Lessing's *Briefing For A Descent Into Hell*, and John Fowles' *The Magus* but forms of the Hades Journey? Each of those stories is like a trapdoor through which we are invited to descend. And whatever the particular character of the events awaiting us there, we are, at the same time, being drawn into deeper imaginative acquaintance with what was once called the Underworld or the Otherworld, but which was courageously explored during the course of last century as the archetypal structure of the unconscious mind.

The prevailing spirit of our time is so identified with the actions and ambitions of the conscious ego that we tend to forget how much of the business of living is almost entirely the duty of the unconscious. The various metabolic processes of the body, on which our lives depend, go about their business with scarcely a moment's conscious thought; even when we are wide awake much of the information reaching us from outside is registered not in the conscious but the unconscious mind; and for a third part of every day we give ourselves to sleep. It has been calculated that we spend sixteen years of our life in the secluded world of dream, which is such a considerable investment of time that we might fairly regard ourselves as amphibious (that is, toad-like) creatures, equally at home in both conscious and unconscious worlds, and deeply in need of both. It's possible, of course, to regard dreams as merely a form of psychic excretion, a clearing of the system ready for a new day; but both the wisdom of many cultures and the witness of a host of individuals insist there is a richer story to tell about them – that dreams too are helpful trapdoors opening on the underworld of the unconscious, which is the deep ground of the Imagination.

Because they remain impenetrably private experiences, all accounts of dreams are inevitably anecdotal, and may concern only the dreamer. And not all dreams, of course, are pleasant. Yet the archetypal psychologist James Hillman insists that our dreams mean well by us, and if we share that view we can begin to see them as profitable conversations held with our deepest being in an arena beyond the narrow claims and control of the conscious ego. They can also be lively oracles of change.

"In dreams," said Yeats, "begins responsibility," and this has certainly been my own experience. It was a powerful and disturbing dream of Yeats which first summoned me out of the relative security of full-time teaching and demanded that I respond to the call of the writing life – a call which had rung clearly throughout my youth but from which I had beaten a depressing retreat since studying English literature among some ferocious intellects at Cambridge. Much later, one of the key formative influences on my novel *The Chymical Wedding* was an enlarging dream which came at a time when I had failed to find what I believed to be a satisfactory answer to a child's demand to know what could be done about the terrifying fact that the world was imminently threatened by nuclear warfare. By giving that dream to the narrator of the novel I sought to put it out into the world, hoping to draw attention to the archetypal issues which, I had come to believe, had a bearing on that urgent question. And I might never have come to write my latest novel at all, had it not been for the impact of a dream so powerful that my Imagination worked with it for many years until it became the starting point for *The Water Theatre* and the matrix from which the whole novel gradually emerged.

Unsurprisingly, therefore, I believe that our adventures in the underworld of dream are not only occasions for self-examination but can also prove to be a source of inspiration. But because they cannot be publicly observed and are so fugitive in their nature, they are frequently disregarded or undervalued, as is also the case with other significant dimensions of our experience – dimensions to which the poet in us may have clearer access than the abstract thinker.

We have four principal functions by which we apprehend the world, and thinking certainly figures among them; but so does feeling (by which I mean not raw emotion but a rational way of evaluating experiences), and we would be utterly lost without the faculties of our five senses; but don't we also rely on intuition, however irrational it may seem, as a way of grasping the meaning in situations without prior conceptualisation? At those times when we fire on all four cylinders at once, then we are fully alive – alive in all our senses, thinking clearly, feeling vividly, and open to other frequencies of intelligence through our intuitive power. That fullness of being is, for me, the vital activity of the Imagination by which we give shape and coherence to our world, and charge our experience with meaning and value. One might also describe it, therefore, as the creative activation of the soul – though I use that word, without invoking any particular religious creed, as the denominator of a perspective on life which is distinguishable from that of the executive ego. And to those sceptical readers who question the reality of the soul on the grounds that there is no objectively demonstrable proof of its existence, let me suggest that there is no demonstrable proof of the ego's existence either, but can anyone doubt that it makes its presence felt in the world?

This is the kind of creative energy of which Yeats was speaking when he talked of the necessary revolt of the soul against the intellect, and creative individuals, whether artists or scientists, have always understood this power of the Imagination – William Blake, for instance who declared that Imagination is "the human existence itself"; Samuel Taylor Coleridge who insisted that "the imagination is the prime agent of human perception" and Albert Einstein who declared, "Imagination is more important than knowledge. Knowledge is limited. Imagination encircles the world." Because imaginative activity has its roots in our unconscious life, it is informed by intelligence from sources deeper and wider than mere ingenuity. Also, in a sense inimical to the taste for novelty and modern ideas of progress, its capacity for original creation relates back to the creative origins of life itself and can, as I suggested a moment ago, be more completely understood as the work of the soul than of the unassisted intellect.

Even as I write this, however, I hear a voice over my shoulder muttering, "This high talk of Imagination and the Unconscious, of Soul and Otherworld, is all very well, but if the seed-bed of creativity lies deep in the unconscious, how is anyone supposed to find a way down there to access what it has to say?"

Well, as I hope I've shown, our dreams can provide one entrance to the underworld, but there are others. A while ago, as part of my work with the Pushkin Trust, I was asked to lead a workshop on the theme 'What do we mean by Creativity?' Rather than pinning it down with abstract definitions, we decided to stalk it like a natural history unit, looking for the kind of habitat in which it thrives, and spotting things likely to scare that wild creature away.

The latter were quickly identified: authority figures who keep it under critical scrutiny, either outwardly in our lives, or pontifical ghosts we have internalised from bad experiences in the past. Then there are oppressive expectations which can induce an inhibiting fear of failure or ridicule. And rife in the culture as a whole are certain tendencies which restrict the free range of the creative Imagination. Among those are demands to comply with conventional patterns of thought, such as reductionism, that overly pragmatic insistence on 'nothing-but-ness' with its consequent demeaning of the sense of wonder and mystery; literalism, which is an inability to see through the surface of things for lack of a metaphorical sense of experience; and scientism, the tendency to validate only that which can be quantified, replicated and evidentially proved – criteria which leave little room for such important and incommensurable aspects of our lives as, for example, love. The presence of any of these factors can drive creativity back into hiding, maybe beyond recall.

But when and where do creative thoughts arrive most easily? Some answers were: in the bath, out walking, while travelling, during hypnogogic moments while falling asleep or hypnopompic moments on waking. All of these are states of reverie where new associations of thought and imagery are freed to form without censorship or obedience to conventions. They are liminal states – on the threshold, neither here nor there, betwixt and between, and many artists deliberately try to seek them out. Thus John Keats (who celebrated what he called Shakespeare's "negative capability," his readiness to live "in uncertainties, mysteries and doubts without any irritable reaching after fact and reason") used to try and trick himself into creative activity by dressing to go out, opening the door, then rushing back to his desk and starting to write.

Creative ideas seem to come in moments when the customary

habits of thought have been disinhibited in ways that permit entry to fresh possibilities. In such conditions of diffused focus, often heightened by sensory awareness (the play of light, the warmth of bathwater), new patterns emerge out of a soft, receptive chaos in which one is tolerant of diversity and ambiguity, even of contradiction. Such a state can, of course, be a vulnerable and sometimes deranging condition, particularly when life has visited a grievous affliction on us – a defeat, an illness, a bereavement or breakdown, some forced descent into a dark underworld that throws us into a gruelling degree of confusion, but which may eventually, though not always, prove generative of new endeavour. Thus much of my own work as a novelist remains an attempt to make sense in fictional terms of a difficult and involuntary journey to the interior which I was obliged to undertake while enduring such an ordeal many years ago as a result of the simultaneous collapse of my first marriage and my masculine ego.

Though I spoke earlier of the active Imagination in terms of experiencing "a fullness of being," at this point I recall, paradoxically, that the more I reflect on such transformative, liminal experiences (and on the ways in which they might relate to those precious moments at my desk when I feel more like a pipeline than an engineer,) the less they feel to speak of 'fullness' than of a transitory *emptiness* of being. Such, it seems to me, is the essential nature of those moments – moments scarcely of time at all – when one has become, beyond conscious volition, a vacant, receptive space, tuned into new frequencies through which something fresh and unanticipated can enter and find form. To go back to the old story with which I began, this state of imminently creative emptiness is the shaft down which the prince descends, not knowing quite what he will find. Peter Brook writes cogently about the vital importance of 'The Empty Space' as the arena of imaginative invention and discovery in theatre; and one of my own mentors, the poet George Barker (who was the uncle of John Fairfax), catches the spirit of it in this poem from *Villa Stellar:*

> Not in the poet is the poem or
> even the poetry. It is hiding behind
> a broken wall or a geranium
> or walking around pretending to be blind
> seeking a home that it cannot find.
>
> Into the ego that has emptied out
> everything except its abstract being
> and left only a shell, the poem then
> moves silently, foreseeing
> its purpose is to haunt the shell like singing.

In that alert state of emptiness it is as if the illusory veil or boundary which seems to separate us from all else is momentarily suspended and there is no division between inner and outer, conscious and unconscious, perceiver and perceived, the poet and the poem. Space itself has become a frictionless medium where all things co-inhere, and the Imagination apprehends and communicates that mutuality of being so feelingly that it is not only the prime agent of perception, it is the agency of compassion too.

None of this is to imply, of course, that one can simply sit back waiting for the poem or novel to arrive. Far from it, and the delicate nature of the operation which takes place beyond the usual conscious control of writers yet within the receptive gravitational field of their being, is caught in the poem *Soror Mystica*[1] by John Moat, who understands these things well:

[1] From *A Fabrication of Gold* (The Write Factor, 2011)

At the outset
It is a moment too soon
One could not say anything for certain
She has her finger to her lips
The sign of caution.

When the work is under way
One cannot risk uttering a word
The least distraction and the moment might be missed
She has her finger to her lips
The sign of concentration.

At the conclusion
It is already too late
The moment can never be repeated
She has her finger to her lips
The sign of the secret.

So writers must work, and keep on working carefully, at their craft. "Without unceasing Practice nothing is gained," said William Blake; "Practice is Art." But perhaps such work is a way of tuning oneself like an instrument on which language and the Imagination can perform what they need to say. And maybe in that way the writer escapes the ego's sovereignty and enters the service of a larger consciousness of which personal consciousness is but a filament?

"Not I but the wind that blows through me," D. H. Lawrence declared, and to the Greeks the wind was *anemos*, which also meant breath, and from that word the Romans derived *animus* and *anima*, spirit and soul. The Latin for breath was *spiritus* and, for breathing, *aspiratio*, to which is related inspiration, for to breathe in was to inspire.

But their word for what we call inspiration was *afflatus*, the breath or wind of the Muse or a God, and in the traditions of India, the word *Atman*, apart from referring to soul, can also mean wind or breath. So is something universal indicated here – an acknowledgment that when the Imagination is fully activated and one finds oneself in the creative state of inspiration, one is drawing breath from a universal source in order to express it – that is, to breathe it out – in personal terms?

Who knows? Such matters remain an essential part of the wonder and mystery of language and the potential for imaginative activity with which each of us arrives in this world. What I do know is that this essay, like others in this book, speaks for, and from, a way of relating to the Imagination which may be as old as poetry itself. Its allegiance is to an ancient wisdom tradition no longer fashionable in a time when our world is largely dominated by the activity of the ascendant left-brain, which has different priorities of its own – priorities which already, as Iain McGilchrist argues in his book *The Master and His Emissary*, have increasingly corrosive effects on our personal and cultural lives. It's also a time when, as Blake lamented in his own day, such wisdom is most often to be found in "that desolate market where none come to buy." But then that tradition of the Imagination, which is profoundly indigenous to vernacular culture as well as finding expression in the arts, is not, and has never been, a saleable commodity. Like the folktales which have preserved memories of its wisdom down the centuries, it's an inalienable part of our birth-right heritage, freely available to everyone and, for that reason among many others, is valued pricelessly among those who have come to care deeply for what it has to say.

TWO POEMS

Colette Bryce

The White Page

I stepped from my skis and stumbled in, like childhood,
knee deep, waist deep, chest deep, falling
for the sake of being caught
in its grip.

It was crisp and strangely dry and I thought: I could drop
here and sleep in my own shape, happily,
as the hare fits
to its form.

I could lie undiscovered like a fossil in a rock
until a hammer's gentle knock might split
it open; warm
and safe

in a wordless place (the snowfall's simple increase), and finally
drift into the dream of white from which
there is no way back
nor out.

I placed myself in that cold case, like an instrument into velvet,
and slept.

The Poetry Bug

is a moon-pale, lumpish creature
parcelled in translucent skin
papery as filo pastry
patterned faint as a fingerprint
is quite without face or feature
ear or eye or snout
has eight root-like
tentacles or feelers, rough
like knuckly tusks of ginger
clustered at the front.

Invisible to the naked eye
monstrous in microscopy
it loves the lovers' bed or couch
pillow, quilt or duvet
and feeds, *thrives* I should say
on human scurf and dander
indeed, is never happier
than feasting on the dust
of love's shucked husk,
the micro-detritus of us.

SECRET FIRE

Patrick Harpur

EVEN THOSE OF us who hold a high Romantic view of Imagination find it hard to picture what it was, for instance, to the melancholic magus, Marsilio Ficino, whose famous academy was the beating heart of Florence, as Florence was the heart of the Renaissance. For him, as for his Neoplatonic mentors, the cosmos was the realm of Imagination itself through which the stars like archetypes – like gods – moved, moving us with the emanations of their *vis imaginativa*, imaginative power. Ficino's attempts to net that power through natural magic are but hazily documented. Yet they certainly involved a combination of incantation and music, sacred talismans and scents and colours, to create an environment so 'sympathetic' to the planetary influences, whether Venereal or Jovial, Saturnine or Solar, that they were as if automatically drawn down, transforming the individual magus or used by him to transform others. Ficino's follower, the English magus John Dee, similarly speaks of directing the stars' *effluvia* into the "imaginative spirit" where they coalesce more intensely, he says, "as in a mirror, show us wonders and work wonders within us" – a marvellous depiction of the psyche as a kind of lens, concentrating and fusing the emanations of its own unconscious archetypes, pictured as both planets and gods.

I've begun with Ficino and Dee because I want to emphasise, firstly, that it is a modern eccentricity to think of Imagination as being solely contained within us; and, secondly, that far from being some vague abstraction, it is a concrete theurgical power such as the Neoplatonists believed could bring statues to life.

What Ficino and Dee consciously invoked, Jacob Boehme experienced spontaneously when his eye happened to fall one day on a burnished pewter dish, which reflected the sunlight with such splendour (his friend Abraham von Franckenburg reported) that "he fell into an inward ecstasy and was suddenly able to gaze into the deepest foundations of the world." This happened in 1600, around the time of the scientific revolution when we ceased to take our congruence with Nature for granted, as Ficino did, and began to experience it as wholly separate from ourselves. Boehme shows his modern cast of mind when he thought that his vision must be only *phantasia*, a delusion easily banished by going outside. But when he walked out into the green fields, he found himself gazing into the very heart of things, down to the inner life of the smallest blade of grass, as if he were not simply observing Nature but intimately participating in it – as if his particular Imagination reflected a universal Imagination, like Wordsworth in the poetic trance of 'Tintern Abbey,' seeing "into the life of things." Boehme's vision of Nature is the first of its kind that I'm aware of. Although it still occurs, especially among poets and painters, it's rare. But it may once have been simply the way we all experienced the world, before we were cruelly divided from it.

Boehme did not make art out of his experience but theology. He asserted that the whole cosmos was powered by Imagination, the creative energy of God himself. It was left to William Blake to make this view into poetry, and to call forth 'Jesus the Imagination' out of Boehme's alchemical belief that we should transmute ourselves through Imagination into an image of Christ; or, more precisely, to set our souls to imagining into Christ, as God imagines into the soul. Blake was able in the crucible of Imagination to forge us back into unity with the world: "To the eyes of a man of Imagination, Nature is Imagination itself."

Ficino and Dee, Boehme and Blake, are all key links in what the alchemists called the Golden Chain, which stretched back to Plato and the Neoplatonists via the alchemists and Hermetic philosophers, and which advanced through the Romantic poets, up to and including Yeats, Eliot and Ted Hughes, to the depth psychology of Jung and James Hillman. I'm sure John Moat won't mind if I place him, too, in this tradition which was often thought of by the prevailing orthodoxies – whether of Church or Science – as 'secret' or 'occult'. But really it is only occult, or hidden, because it is elusive and subtle. The secret it bears is, like the 'secret fire' of alchemy, the secret of Imagination and its exaltation over Reason as the chief faculty of the soul. It's an open secret because, even when we know it, it remains - as John reminds us in his essay 'The Gist of Arvon' – a mystery. And, moreover, even if not Christian, certainly and always a sacred mystery. Like all the great portmanteau words, such as love, God, mind, etc., Imagination can be defined endlessly. Indeed, it is as bottomless as Heraclitus' psyche, whose end you couldn't find "though you travelled every path, so deep is its measure."

I wonder that we ever came to use the word Imagination so trivially, as we commonly do today – as a quality endearing in children as long as it doesn't become over-active; as a simple associative mechanism, enabling us to picture things absent to the senses; and as an ability to make things up. I prefer to call this ability 'fancy,' as Coleridge did (following Boehme's phantasia) and to distinguish it sharply from Imagination proper which, as he reminds us, is something more thunderous: "the living power and prime agent of all human perception, and... a repetition in the finite mind of the eternal I AM."

This, I take it, is what John means by Imagination and what, I suppose, all proper poets mean by it. It means nothing less than belief in a great ocean of images which exists quite separately from us, a dynamic and autonomous Otherworld, out of which, I dare say, we are born and to which we return at death. Occasionally, like Shelley's traveller in an antique land, we are confronted by Ozymandian images more kingly than the rest – Platonic Forms or archetypes around which lesser images cluster like daimons in the retinue of a god. Indeed, the notion of gods does greater justice to such supernatural images than any abstract concept, not because we personify them but because Imagination, it seems, prefers to come to us in the first instance as persons – persons such as the heroes, daimons and gods who interact in those unauthored narratives we call myths.

Always individual, always the same – "as alike as the lines on the palm of the hand," says Ted Hughes – myths underwrite whatever view of reality we hold dear. When Proclus suggested that myths are composed by the daimons who shape our lives – in other words, that the daimons who inhabit myths also invented them – he supplied us with a superlative metaphor for the way myths generate themselves out of Imagination. Moreover, he was suggesting that, as Yeats comments, "there is some one myth for every man which, if we but knew it, would make us understand all he did and thought." There is in our lives, as John rightly divines, a blueprint with an intention, or (as Plato has it) a *paradeigma* with a *telos* carried for us by the personal daimon.

Myth is not the opposite of reality, as modernity would have us believe; rather, as Isaiah Berlin remarks, myth is what gives us our sense of reality. "These things never happened," says Sallust sublimely, "they are always." If we deny myth, we deny it in a manner already laid down by myth. What Jung said of his archetypes holds true of the myths and their gods: "All we know is that we seem unable to imagine without them... If we invent them, then we invent them according to the patterns they lay down." In other words we can't see the world except through some imaginative framework, some perspective. Some myth. The world we see is the myth we are in. We can have a choice of what myth we'll look through, but we do not, as scientism wishes us to believe, have a choice of no myth at all. But to believe that our myth about the world is in fact the only world is to mistake, as it is often said these days, the map for the territory. It is the sin of literalism.

When Blake saw the sun, not as "a round disk of fire somewhat like a Guinea," but as "an Innumerable company of the Heavenly host crying 'Holy, holy, holy is the Lord God Almighty,'" he was asserting the priority of the mythopoeic Imagination over perception. He was practising what he called 'double vision':

> This life's dim windows of the Soul
> Distorts the Heavens from Pole to Pole
> And leads you to believe a lie
> When you see with, not thro' the eye.

To see *with* the eye alone is to see the world as it appears; to see *through* the eye is to see the world as it is. It is the difference between mere eyesight and deeper vision; between seeing only the literal and seeing beyond the literal to the metaphorical. For example:

> With my inward eye 'tis an old Man grey;
> With my outward, a Thistle across my way.

The thistle we see with the eye, then, becomes an old man when we see through it. To see only a thistle is literalism; but, equally, to see only an "old Man grey" is literalism of another sort, a turning of poetic vision into illusion or hallucination. To imagine is not to lose sight of the thistle even as we are seeing the old man. We must see the dryad in the oak, certainly, but not forget the oak. This perpetual sense of metaphor – of two worlds interpenetrating – is the art of Imagination.

Plato famously argued that art is a bad thing because it merely copies objects in Nature – which are themselves copies of the eternal Forms in the intelligible world of *Nous*. Art is only a copy of a copy and therefore less real than the natural world we see around us. Plotinus easily disposed of this notion, and in an interesting way. While natural objects are indeed imitations of the Forms, he says, "the arts do not simply imitate what they see but re-ascend to those principles (*logoi*) from which Nature herself is derived." He takes it for granted, we notice, that there is an imaginative ground of being which underlies both the collective natural world and us as individuals. So, no matter how prosaic and profane the object – a piece of fruit, say, or a pair of boots – they become in the hands of a Cézanne or a van Gogh transparent to the sacred Form of fruit or boot. They glow with independent, 'ensouled' life. The work of art embodies the very double vision required to view it aright. It is a marriage of literal and metaphorical, subject and object, consciousness and the unconscious, personal and impersonal, particular and universal – there is no boundary the work of art, like a daimon, cannot straddle.

Just as Imagination is analogous to Jung's collective unconscious – that "alien country outside the ego" – so both find their prototype in Plato's Soul of the World. Plotinus and his fellow Neoplatonists elevated soul to the very stuff of reality. It is, said Plotinus, "the cosmic force that unifies, organises, sustains and controls every aspect of the world." In short, the whole cosmos is ensouled and everything is connected in the world-soul. This, of course, is exactly what tribal cultures believe – the cultures we pejoratively call 'animistic'. For them, everything has a soul, every rock and tree and stream is daimon-ridden, every place has a genius, as if the whole of Nature were transparent to the Soul of the World. According to the Neoplatonists, and to all members of the Golden Chain, we humans have a special and central position because, while we are each only one soul among many, a single drop in the ocean of the world-soul, we also have capacity to embrace the whole of the world-soul. We are microcosms in relation to the macrocosm – that is, little worlds analogous to the great world. Our souls are individual manifestations of the collective Soul of the World, yet, paradoxically, they also at some profound level contain it, just as Jung thought we contained a collective unconscious.

According to the Neoplatonic model of reality, then, we are bound to consider the disconcerting notion (commonplace to any self-respecting Buddhist) that soul manifests primarily as images; that image is therefore the ground of reality; that image is real as long as it is not taken literally; that, as individual manifestations of the Soul of the World, we too are images. "Our thoughts are not, as we suppose, the deep," Yeats reminds us, "but a little foam upon the deep." Even our bodies are not literal – material, of course, just as soul and its daimons are both material and spiritual; but not literal. It has simply been the misfortune of matter in our age to be the chief bearer of the literalistic perspective.

John Moat is one of the few people in our provincial age to have noticed that one of the enterprises which best embodies the concrete, transforming power of Imagination is alchemy – the quest not for 'common gold' but for some more mysterious 'philosophical gold.' We have Jung to thank for the insight that alchemy is far from being a sort of primitive chemistry; it is a profound science of the soul – what he called "the historical counterpart of [his] own psychology of the unconscious." At first, he saw that the constituents of the alchemical process, such as mercury and sulphur, King and Queen, sun and moon which were separated and combined in stages variously named conjunction, mortification, putrefaction, sublimation, so forth – all subsumed under the symphonic sweep of three greater movements: Blackness, Whiteness and Redness – were hallucinatory projections from the unconscious on to 'our matter,' sealed up in the 'Hermetic egg.' But he changed his mind when he came across an "astounding definition" in Martin Ruland's 1622 *Lexicon of Alchemy*: "Imagination is the star (*astrum*) in man, the celestial or supercelestial body."

He saw at once that the *Magnum Opus*, or Great Work, was not a series of "immaterial phantoms" but something actual, even corporeal, like a 'subtle body.' Imagination, he wrote, "is perhaps the most important key to the understanding of the Opus." The "imaginal world" (as the Islamic scholar, Henri Corbin, calls it) lies between subject and object, psyche and matter, so that when the alchemists asserted that their Art is nothing other than to transform their 'prime matter' into the Philosophers' Stone via a 'secret fire', Jung understood this as the psyche of the alchemist being transformed by Imagination into its Self.

But isn't this imaginal realm precisely the one into which we are all initiated by intensely creative activity, a realm where material processes and psychic change interpenetrate, like magic?

"He is all things, who was but one… in him are the four elements, and yet himself is no element; he is spirit, and he hath a body; he is a man, who yet acts the part of a woman… He is life yet kills all things… he flyeth from the Fire, yet Fire is made of him; he is water, yet wets not…" Who is this strange, contradictory god-like being whom the alchemist Michael Sendivogius is trying to describe? The Tao (or Dao)? Soul? Imagination?

John will recognise him as perhaps all of these. He (or she, or it) is the presiding spirit of the Great Work – Hermes' shadowy younger brother, Mercurius. As concrete as the quicksilver running through the veins of the earth and as elusive as the Soul of the World, Mercurius encompasses all paradoxes. He is at once the prime matter, secret fire and Stone ("that is no stone," as the alchemists always helpfully add). Just as distillation heats the primal fluid so that it vaporises into gas (the soul leaving the body of 'our matter'); just as the gas cools and condenses back into a more pure fluid, which is fed back – refluxed – into the original fluid (the purified soul returns to the putrefying body, and revives it,) so Mercurius distils himself out of himself in a sublime metaphor for the dynamic, self-circling, self-delighting, forever changing (yet always the same) Imagination. Not the least aim of the Great Work, therefore, is to free the soul – not from the grossness of matter so much as from the grossness of the literalism that matter carries. In this way matter becomes transparent to soul in that 'subtle body' which Jung discovered Imagination to be, and Imagination is delivered into that free play so essential to the soul's health.

The Work, like life, is an imaginative quest. The promise of the Stone is necessary to embolden us to embark on it. But in truth the goal changes on the way as if the Way itself, transforming us as we go along, were the meaning of the quest. So, off we go…

All the little household gods
Have started crying, but say
Good-bye now, and put to sea.
Farewell, dear friend, farewell: may
Hermes, master of the roads,
And the four dwarf Kabiri,
Protect and serve you always;
And may the Ancient of Days
Provide for all you must do
His invisible guidance,
Lifting up, friend, upon you
The light of His countenance.

W.H. Auden *Atlantis*

THE SWEET VOICE OF REASON

LINDA PROUD

"Lord, when someone meets you in a Moment of Vision, is it through the soul (psyche) that they see, or is it through the spirit (pneuma)?' The Teacher answered, 'It is neither through the soul nor the spirit, but the house between the two which sees the vision." *[Gnostic] Gospel of Mary.*

ONCE UPON A time in the land of childhood, a little girl was colouring in a picture of Santa Claus and his reindeer, putting the paint down where she wanted to. She was making a big red blob in the region of Rudolf's nose when her father came along and said, "No, not like that." He put her on his knee, took hold of her hand and showed her how to paint within the lines. She watched fascinated as, guided by her father's firm hand, her brush filled in the outlines with paint. She had taken a step. *Tekhne* had begun and she was now on course to acquire the skills of art. Did she have a taste of that, or did she just feel cross? Restricted. Hobbled. Her days of freedom over, her creativity circumscribed by those who draw the lines?

As I remember, she felt both.

In the beginning there was One; next thing there were Two. Life as we know it (untranscendent, everyday mortality) is composed of contraries: male-female, good-bad, right-wrong, yin-yang, left brain-right brain, sun-moon, soul-spirit, head and heart. The word 'versus' comes into play a lot. Reason has several 'opposites' – Imagination, irrationality, faith, belief, revelation – and amongst creative types is always the bad guy. Guy. Definitely male, is Reason, despite her medieval period as a goddess[1]. Reason spoils our dreams, oppresses our creativity, puts the bit in our mouth, binds our feet, poops on our parties. Reason is a scientist in a white lab coat, all scepticism and dourness in the face of our wilder delusions, such as magic, fairies, UFOs and religion.

In ancient days it was easier to understand and define reason for then it was normal to believe in the sacred. According to the Pythagoreans, reason links the immortal part of the human mind (psyche) with the divine order of the cosmos. Plato considered reason to be the monarch which should rule over the other parts, such as spiritedness (thumous) and the emotions. (Hackles begin to rise here, but let's hear the man out; after all, we're only getting irritated by the idea of being ruled over by the divine part of our own minds.) Aristotle defined a happy life as that lived consistently in accordance with reason. For Plotinus reason is both the provider of form to material things, and the light which guides individual souls back to their source.

Such thinking governed Arabic and Western philosophy until modern times, when a new understanding separated man from the cosmos, a process which led to a sense of the sacred being considered 'irrational.' When Descartes introduced reason (i.e. methodological scepticism) as the only certain way to knowledge, it was the beginning of our own age, the Age of Me. Separated from the world, Man was free to study things objectively, for he was not those things. (Now, of course, he's becoming confounded as he comes to understand that those things, those particles, are affected by his watching them.)

---

[1] According to CS Lewis in *The Discarded Image*, Reason is *intelligentia obumbrata*, the shadow of angelic nature in man. A trace of her, he says, remains in the modern use of 'reasonable'. The ancient Greek Pallas Athene and Roman Minerva, both goddesses of wisdom, presided over poetry. Minerva's name means 'she who measures.' Both are often depicted in armour, carrying a sword symbolising 'the blade of reason.' A goddess, then, but with nothing girly about her.

By the time of the so-called Enlightenment, Reason had been divested of her femininity, plucked out of her place in the cosmos (just below the Primum Mobile), and put to inventing machines and exploitative economic systems.

The main difference between modern and ancient ideas of reason is that moderns consider it a function of the brain, a type of thought, while the ancients considered it a faculty of mind. These days 'reason' seems to mean whatever any particular philosopher wants it to mean. There are types of reason, don't you know, the type used by a scientist and the type used by an artist, which apparently are not the same. Logic. Deduction. Judgement. Ability to solve Sudoku. You name it. One philosopher has gone so far as to say that understanding reason is so difficult that it takes an expert to do it (himself, presumably). Reading through the various definitions is a quick way to fuddle the brain. Is it that we can't use reason to define itself but can only be aware of it in action?

One of the main aspects of modern reason (or science) is that conclusions reached by logic and deduction are considered more certain than sense perceptions. That must be true. Take the example of spontaneous generation. It was by his senses that the seventeenth century chemist, Jean Baptista van Helmont, observed that, "if one presses a dirty shirt into the opening of a vessel containing grains of wheat, the ferment from the dirty shirt does not modify the smell of the grain but gives rise to the transmutation of the wheat into mice after about twenty-one days."

If you're going to rely on your senses, you absolutely have to have recourse to doubt and scepticism. And that's the kind of reason we think of today when we use the word; the reason which dispels ignorance. That would be fine if science didn't dismiss any form of perception other than through the senses or reason. The visionary, the inspired, the divinely mad, they suggest, should be silenced. Medicated.

Science and art have become divided and now often occupy hostile camps. Artists see scientists as in the pay of Big Pharma; scientists see anyone who won't recognise the cosmos as a place of spinning lumps of rock or clouds of gas as deluded. We are talking extremes here, but those extremes exist and it seems the polarisation is increasing until there is a kind of Civil War of the mind going on, with brother pitched against brother. Someone who in every other respect is your friend suddenly turns on you snarling when you use a pendulum to choose between Cornflakes and Weetabix; or you turn on them snarling when they say that a foetus in a late abortion feels no pain.

Because of its usurpation by positivists, reason has become synonymous with the father figure who represses our feminine side, a bloody-mawed Cronos chewing on the flesh of his children (creative ideas) and spitting out their bones. He wags his finger, tells us to do something useful with our lives, and sneers at whatever we hold dear: alternative medicine, astrology, any kind of faith or ritual. This universe, he says with no smile on his face, is mechanical and has no meaning. Beauty is just the activation of the pleasure receptors in the brain, is subjective and therefore untrue.

In the view of the artist and poet, then, it is Reason who experiments on animals, who culls badgers, puts fluoride in the water and builds nuclear power stations. Reason always, always knows best. And so we do everything we can to stimulate Imagination – take creative writing courses, listen to music, go for long walks, visit art galleries, write to the sound of aeolian harps while incense burns – as if Imagination has been shut in a cellar of the mind and needs to be freed (conjured, even).

But is this picture true, or have we have confused reason with some other force? Let us call it 'negativity' for short and set it quietly to one side.

So what is reason, and what does it mean for the writer? Because without reason we are not merely irrational, we are insane, unable to string a sentence or compose a paragraph or write anything comprehensible. Reason, the most precious instrument in the toolkit, thought of as 'versus Imagination' has become overlooked and unacknowledged. It takes a poet to understand reason, because what reason is *not* is logical positivism. It is not empirical; it does not depend on the senses; it is not materialist; it does not depend on sense perception. Reason is the mind's eye, able to judge and discern, but it is not harsh. Reason is gentle. Reason is sweet.

Interestingly, any poet writing on the subject of Reason or the Imagination (notably Shelley, *In Defence of Poetry*, and Coleridge, *Biographia Literaria*) writes about creativity in the precise, abstract language of philosophy. Those essays are perfectly structured masterpieces of reason. When the poet tries to understand and explain what happens in writing, he becomes very rational indeed. And that's a big hint about what Reason is.

Let's go back to the ancients. Socrates, the father of Reason who could spear his interlocutors with questions that caused them, to put it nicely, to realise their own ignorance, old Socrates had a daimon; more correctly, a *daimonion* (a 'divine something') that was an inner voice that warned him but never advised him. It seems his daimon had but one word, which was "No!"

Plutarch tells more of the story in the *Moralia*. When Socrates was born, his father was told that the boy would never need formal education but would be guided in wisdom. Socrates always trusted his inner promptings. Once on a walk with friends he suddenly changed direction. Some younger men kept to the original way just to confute Socrates's daimon but they were met by a herd of filthy swine, too many for the street to contain, and came out of the encounter pretty filthy themselves.

Some of his contemporaries said that Socrates' daimon was nothing but a sneeze, now to the right, now to the left, the direction of the sneeze being significant. It was not a sneeze, however, nor an apparition, but a sensible perception of a voice, that is, not a physical voice but as in a dream when we have fancies and apprehensions of words which make us imagine that we hear someone speak.

The implication is that we all have a daimon (which some equate with Guardian Angel) but we either don't hear what it says, or we ignore it. Socrates could hear his daimon even in the bustle of the day because he was quiet within. And, most importantly, he did what the daimon told him. If the daimon is but a name for Reason, it seems that Reason is strengthened by obedience.

Obedience! What a word! Out come the whips and chains of Imagination again, to picture Reason as a prison guard bringing his whimpering victims to heel. But this is not what Socrates is telling us; he is not saying, "Obey the dictates of Reason or you will be punished!" He's saying, "If you want wisdom, do as this spirit suggests."

You will not be punished if you ignore the daimon (although you may come out of the alley somewhat smellier than when you went in) you will just be left in ignorance.

In the *First Book of Kings* in the Old Testament is the story of Elijah. He is on the run from Jezebel, who is furious that he has threatened her priests with death, and in the wilderness he falls asleep under a juniper tree, praying for death himself because he considers himself a failure. He is twice woken by an angel, who gives him enough food to fortify him on a journey to Mount Horeb. Later, on the sacred mountain, Elijah takes shelter in a cave, where "the word of the Lord came to him" and told him to stand upon the mount before the Lord. Which he did. "And, behold, the Lord passed by, and a great and strong wind rent the mountains, and brake in pieces the rocks before the Lord; but the Lord was not in the wind: and after the wind an earthquake; but the Lord was not in the earthquake: And after the earthquake a fire; but the Lord was not in the fire: and after the fire a still small voice."

This story is the source of the hymn by John Greenleaf Whittier, 'Dear Lord and Father of Mankind,' so popular for that one, softly-sung line at the end, "O still, small voice of calm."

Elijah hears at least three kinds of divine message: the angel, the voice of the Lord, and the Lord himself. In each case, he does what he's told. He equivocates, mumbles and moans, but he does it. The Old Testament is rather full of this kind of tetchy communication between Man and the Divine: the burning bush, Abraham, Job, Jonah, Noah, Jacob and his dreams. Obviously it was not unusual in those days to have conversations with God, and it certainly wasn't considered delusional.

There was a renowned rabbi in the sixteenth century, called Joseph Karo, whose book of laws is still in use today. For fifty years he kept a journal recording the visits of an angelic being he called the 'Maggid' (itinerant preacher). Unlike Socrates' daimon, the Maggid had much to say, mostly about how Karo lived his life. The rabbi was told-off for his wrongdoings, exhorted to study the *Kabbala*, to asceticism and good deeds. He was told to be gentle, to be patient, to be modest, devout, and to say his prayers. He got some of the "No!" treatment when it came to an extra glass of wine or eating meat. When Karo did not obey, the Maggid sternly warned him, but when satisfied that his student deserved it, the Maggid revealed Kabbalistic interpretations of the Pentateuch.

In our post-Freudian, post-Jungian world we may now describe the Inner Prompter as the subconscious, or active Imagination, or conscience, or inspiration. But what does that mean? The real question is, "Who speaks? And to whom?"

Once I was the ancestral voice of the Father-wisdom, the theosophia that spoke inarticulately through blood and instinct, but articulately through the sibyls, the prophets, the masters. But at the turning-point of time, by that central death and rebirth which was the transformation of transformations, by the open mystery of Golgotha, I was myself transformed. I am that anthroposophia who... is the voice of each one's mind speaking from the depths within himself.
– Owen Barfield, *Unancestral Voice*

Owen Barfield (1898-1997), jurist, philosopher and one of the Inklings, studied the nature of language and human consciousness. In *Poetic Diction – A study in meaning,* he traces the evolution of poetry from ancient times, when words came from without, from the muse or genius or some divinity separate from the poet, to modern times when creativity has become internalised and the poet finds the words within.

In Chapter 6 he describes the two fundamental states of mind of the individual: the creative and the appreciative. We could equally call these Imagination and Reason. Without reason, he says, there would be no speech. "It follows that the poet's power of *expression* will be dependent on the development of the rational principle within himself."

These two moods (inspiration and abstract thinking) are, he says, essentially incompatible with each other. "Inspiration was the only means by which poetry could be written, and the poet himself hardly knew what it was – a kind of divine wind, perhaps, which blew where it listed and might fill his sails at some odd moment after he had whistled for it all day in vain."

Barfield suggests a practical method may be to alternate between Imagination and Reason quickly. Rather than write a whole novel in creative mode, and then edit it in judgement mode, try to get these two things happening more quickly. Then an oscillation starts up and the bird is flying. He quotes an unnamed critic as saying, "To write well of love, a man must be in love, but to correct his writing, he must be out of it again." Thought of like this, it would seem tough to speed up the process, yet it must be done. The subjective and objective view can never be simultaneous, but in rapid alternation or oscillation, the true image begins to arise. We are now approaching that sacred ground which all writers aspire to: where the writer becomes the reader and, while responsible for what appears on the page, is aware of not being its source. A resonation with the divine note has been achieved, and the harmonics which lift a work above the mundane begin to sound.

In *Biographia Literaria*, Coleridge wrote, "Grant me a nature having two contrary forces, the one of which tends to expand infinitely, while the other strives to apprehend or find itself in this infinity, and I will cause the whole world of intelligences… to rise up before you."

What we should be aiming for, then, is full reintegration of the mind. The scientist, learning to trust his intuition (and there are so many examples of scientific discovery being the result of intuition), learning even, perhaps to trust scripture both Eastern and Western, certainly to trust natural law, of which artificial life, genetically modified crops and all the other offerings from science at its maddest (i.e. most irrational), is in clear contravention.

But how do we achieve this wonderful goal? The first thing is to know Reason as she is and to dispense with the false spectre of repression. Listen to her. Obey. Then it becomes easier to hear her. At last we shall see Reason and Imagination as the twin gates to the true, original creativity that is deep and still and fathomless.

The little girl is old now and her father in some new embodiment is being taught to paint within the lines. Now she must be father to herself and guide her thinking and her pen, allowing the creative thought to billow forth, but keeping an objective eye on it, making sure it makes sense, that each word is right in the sentence, that each sentence builds the paragraph, that the paragraph becomes a unit of thought in line with the structure of the piece.

The poet is like the potter, who with one hand forms a pot through discipline and with the other forms it through love. When Reason has the gentleness of Imagination, and Imagination the rigour of Reason, when they listen to each other, and obey, then they twine and spiral upwards in the dance of creation, a *Sinfonia Concertante* for viola and violin.

A PLACE OF CONSTANT SURPRISES

Nick Stimson

WRITING ABOUT THE operation of that canny trickster the Imagination in his essay 'The Gist of Arvon' John Moat says... "...the Imagination is, or is part of, an unguarded generosity. Any endeavour sanctioned by the Imagination will, if true to itself, be proof of this in heart, word and deed. Not by the requisite mission statement printed under your logo, but in spirit pervasive as oxygen in the bloodstream. And so unavoidably inclusive."

The living embodiment of such an imaginative hub, indeed a fully functioning imaginative society, is an extraordinary set up called Hannahs at Seale-Hayne, near Newton Abbot in Devon. On the surface it is a charity – the Dame Hannah Rogers Trust founded some 230 years ago – a charity that works with people who have physical disabilities and sometimes mental disabilities, but Hannahs at Seale-Hayne is way beyond any clichés of worthy basket-weaving or group sing-a-longs. This is an organisation driven by and always celebrating the Imagination – a place of constant surprises.

My first encounter with Hannahs at Seale-Hayne was, I have to admit, as an unwilling and more than somewhat cynical visitor. My wife insisted we pay the place a visit. It's only just down the road and she'd been there several times already and what she'd seen and experienced had greatly impressed her. So along I went, moaning and muttering, not expecting much. And then my eyes were opened.

Once a famous agricultural college Seale-Hayne now comprises a glorious ninety acre site set in the heart of the deep green hill country of South Devon. The jagged tors of Dartmoor to one side and the sea to the other. There's a substantial group of buildings clustered around the grand red brick Victorian edifice of the old college. When the agricultural college finally closed its doors in the mid-noughties, the site was acquired by the Dame Hannah Rogers Trust, who were already running a large and ambitious operation in the nearby town of Ivybridge.

What they have created at Seal-Hayne is a remarkable blueprint, an engine for setting the Imagination into action, for changing lives and the way we understand each other and live together. What goes on here isn't simply about doing good or about clever new therapies, this place is about an all-out assault by the Imagination and it is equally relevant to both the able-bodied and the less able.

Hannahs at Seale-Hayne has set out to bring together a creative community made up of many parts. Everyone who works there, from the refreshingly frank and enthusiastic Chief Executive, Bronwen Hewitt, to the newest recruit is fully signed-up to this adventure; there are no half-measures. What has been achieved there – and they are still only at the start of their journey – is breath-taking in its scope, vision and impact. I was taken on an escorted tour which lasted for several hours and, I suspect, I didn't get much beyond scratching the surface.

First of all the issue. 20% of UK children and adults live with some form of disability. Over 900,000 children in this country live with a disability. That's a large slice of the population, a huge minority most often without a voice or a place in the wider society. An invisible country. There are many stories of disabled young people emerging from care only to live out the rest of their lives lost in an old people's home. The Dame Hannah Roger's Trust seeks to fundamentally alter our relationship with disability.

We all know that freedom of speech is a human right. For one group of people it's not just the daily challenges they face that stand in the way of this basic right. The average 18 month old child has been exposed to 4,380 hours of oral language at a rate of 8 hours a day from birth. A child who uses a communication system and receives speech and language therapy twice a week (for 20-30 minutes) will reach the same amount of language exposure in 84 years... Of course this is a shocking statistic, but what is more worrying is the postcode lottery that dictates if people living with such challenges are eligible for a communication aid, or more poignantly, the funding for it.

What's going on at Hannahs at Seale-Hayne is a massive upheaval in the way we treat, understand, integrate, work with, live with and become one with people who have disabilities. They are taking disability from the concerned and worthy fringe – a place that needn't much bother any of us as we write our plays or novels or poems, or paint our pictures or make our sculptures or create our music, or teach our lessons or make our money or build our dreams in the sky – to a place where we are all on level ground, sharing equal footing, speaking head to head. A place of shared lives. It is their belief that people living with disabilities not only have to be heard, but heard just as much as anyone else and heard until we realise the less able share the same rights, ideas and feelings as the rest of us.

To make this great change Hannahs at Seale Hayne has made its own world and created its own imaginative and fully integrated way to live. You could, if you wanted to be theoretical, look upon this place as an interesting experiment in the integration of those with disability and those without disability. I prefer to see it as practical, hands on way of living for all of us; not an experiment searching for a result, but a society driven by the Imagination, that is on-going and perpetual.

So what's going on there that makes this place so different? For a start what you get isn't an abstract concept but a collective will manifested in actions you can touch, taste, see, smell and hear. There's music-making and performance in abundance. They have a place called the Big Red which is a busy rehearsal and recording studio with state of the art facilities. Guitars, amplifiers, instruments everywhere. The able-bodied and the less able come here to make music together and then perform that music together in front of other people. It's a truly shared journey to which everyone brings their own strengths and needs. There's also a live music venue and club called The Yellow Room where internationally known performers from a range of musical backgrounds come to play. Mike Westbrook's a regular. Again, all abilities work beside each other in shared creative enterprise. There's also a music project called Kagemusha Taiko – dramatic, hypnotic and unforgettable Japanese drumming. Thundering, enthralling drumming. I stumbled in on a group, the big drums raging, the faces of the participants fixed with rhythm and wonder, as was mine.

Perhaps the most remarkable facet of this place is the fact that a whole range of artists and crafts people have chosen to make Hannahs at Seale-Hayne their home. They rent studios and workrooms here, they make their art and their craft here. There are print-makers, painters, photographers, jewellers, even a blacksmith... it's a long list. The rent is set at a knock down rate, an attractive and useful incentive for artists looking for space to work. What they have created here is an artists' community. A group of people who make their living through the Imagination who have come together to work and share their visions and their ideas. (The exact opposite of the all too often stagnant 'artist in residence' situation where the artist seldom gets to do any of their own work – these artists and crafts people at Seale-Hayne are here to do what they do and what they do is prized.)

To be part of this set up each artist has to fully buy into the philosophy of the place – each one giving a proportion of their time to Hannahs. That means their skill or their craft is shared with others. It might sounds like a '60s dream come true – but it works. It feeds the artists and it feeds all those they come into contact with. There's also a terrific gallery where the artists sell their work, a percentage of each sale going to Hannahs. It's a perfect arrangement as the place is always thronged with visitors. The result is that there is art everywhere you look. Work on show created by the resident artists, by those who come on courses and by the less able artists. Sometimes you need to look very carefully to work out which is which and even then there's a chance you might be wrong.

There's a set-up called Camp Mawazo that runs outdoor activities - and who could ignore the splendid outdoors situated here in the heart of Devon? Then there's Hannahs farm teeming with donkeys, ponies, chickens, ducks and goats. There's a sustainable garden project taking shape. There's even something called Sirona Therapeutic Horsemanship that promotes a holistic approach to working with horses.

If anyone's feeling peckish – and you're likely to be feeling more than peckish after walking so far and seeing so much – then you'll also find a very good bistro and a cake shop full of the most luscious and tasty calorie-laden cakes I have ever seen. There are also shops... including the Souk which is like a little Arab market, Serendipity where they sell a wide range of fabrics and a Retro Shop that sells, well, anything retro. Again, a percentage of the takings goes directly to Hannahs and each enterprise works in tune with the place it inhabits.

There's good accommodation for visitors and ambitious plans to expand that accommodation. Seale-Hayne offers plenty of places to have meetings, places to do deals, room to stroll and marvel, have a banquet; you can even get married here if that takes your fancy. There's a Sports Hall where people play hockey, football, basketball, cricket, bowls and lots more besides. There's a hydrotherapy pool, full of mothers and newly-born babies on the day I visited. There are plans to extend the therapies on offer to include a range of complimentary therapies and even a beautician. (And why not? Beauty should be available to everyone.) There's a fitness suite. There's even talk of opening a smart boutique hotel and an upmarket campsite for 'Glampers.' It's a city, a little world all by itself.

Hannahs at Seale-Hayne, as you'll have deduced, is a busy place. Activities everywhere. It's a place where people mix, talk, paint, write, make, sing – they do things together. The car park's full and inquisitive visitors wander around sampling all the delights.

Everyone shares their skills here. That's remarkable. No expectation of wiping your feet and doffing your cap before you visit the high altar of culture. The people here, and I mean *all* the people here, give. They give of themselves. That's the deal. You give, you take, we're all happy. We all move forward. We change the world just a little tiny bit.

I finished the tour and before leaving I took one last look out over the wide lawn that covers the central quadrangle. I see sculptures dotted about everywhere, bright flags with messages on them, a statue of a sheep with DH stamped on its flank, I hear singing coming from somewhere deep inside the building, I hear the sound of the drums pounding, I see people drinking coffee in the spring sunshine, and then I see a tall, bearded man, looking a little like a contemporary Pied Piper, leading a pony through the grounds. Thronging behind him, holding onto the pony and trailing along behind it are a group of laughing, dancing people. I look at the laughing, dancing people again and I realise they are all what an outsider such as myself would describe as disabled.

Bronwen Hewitt is only interested in the doing. In setting up the next venture. In the opening of the next door. Do it right she reckons, and the bills will get paid. So far that is exactly what has happened. This place takes on the impossible and makes it possible. And that, surely, is the first function of the Imagination.

Bronwen Hewitt's recruited a dedicated and oddly joyful team. Everyone I meet is an advocate, a disciple. The cake-makers, the blacksmiths, the artists, the musicians, the technicians and the therapists all share a commonly-held understanding that what they are doing is making the future possible for the less able people with whom they work and in so doing, the less able are making the future possible for *them*. It's a two-way thing this creative commerce at Seale-Hayne, so don't go thinking this is about 'them and us.' The able of mind and body on one side and the less able on the other. It's far from that. The people you see and meet working here, those who are doing the doing and making the making, are often less able themselves. Everywhere you find people of all abilities working side by side. That's part of the process. An on-going, self-making and self-perpetuating process. A truly cybernetic process in that (to quote Wikipedia) it seems to do something like this: "...the system being analysed is involved in a closed signal loop; that is, where action by the system causes some change in its environment and that change is fed to the system via information (feedback) that causes the system to adapt to these new conditions: the system's changes affect its behaviour. This 'circular causal' relationship is necessary and sufficient for a cybernetic perspective."

Hannahs at Seale-Hayne is a place where rules are there to be broken. Not through willfulness or angry rebellion but because a rule doesn't sit easily where the Imagination is waking. It is a place that is both proactive and reactive, that exists to enable all those who come here to be heard, appreciated and to live their lives to the fullest measure. People of all abilities play and dream and quest alongside each other. It's where we forget who is who. Here, as Bronwen Hewitt so aptly describes it, is "a circle of benefit." It is informal like a family, a place of mutual exchange and understanding. Here they are building relationships for life.

As John Moat says in The Gist of Arvon, "The Imagination ... runs an 'open door' policy and is universally inclusive, and the wealth it promises is fulfilment." Like Arvon, Hannahs at Seale-Hayne offers a true and effective alternative to the dead-handed cultural straight-jacket of formal healthcare and jargon-driven education. It is an imaginative spring into the future that can speak to all.

Arvon, a remarkable organisation in its own right, brings together professional writers with people who have an interest in writing. The five-day courses, free of formal educational process and driven by the skills and ideas of the writers are so popular and so successful that it seems like an idea that was surely always with us. Arvon isn't about turning out a host of new writers, it's about changing lives through a direct and sometimes shattering encounter with the Imagination.

What goes on at Hannahs at Seale-Hayne is perhaps more complicated to define. At Arvon there is the immediate and direct chemistry for students (of all ages and all backgrounds) who, at the Arvon centres, come into contact with the writer and the writer's Imagination, and through that encounter they in turn can discover their own Imagination and the power that brings. Hannahs at Seale-Hayne is driven by the shared creative energy of everyone concerned with it. The person serving you coffee may well be disabled though you won't know it, and serving you this coffee might just be a landmark in their life. Here everyone is asked to live and think and work like an artist, tuned to that life-giving encounter that is both the self looking in and the self looking out, both at the same time. This is a societal Imagination, an individual and a group encounter that bond together those involved through shared purpose and the quest for a better future. Artists call it the work of the Imagination. I doubt the waitress in the Bistro or man singing Neil Diamond tunes in the Big Red or the people who eat their breakfasts of a Sunday morning as Mike Westbrook rehearses, or the laughing, dancing people with the pony would see it exactly that way. What they might call it is community, family, place, learning, trusting, understanding, taking risks, valuing.

Hannahs at Seale-Hayne is fighting intolerance and ignorance by inspiring anyone who cares to take the time and drive up the long drive. It is finding ways to overcome the ago-old frustrations of disability – and the best way it has found to do that is by inspiring all, sparking the Imagination, setting it on fire and watching the resulting fireworks light up the darkness. Like the Imagination itself it is not a place of judgment and it sets no limits on what can achieved. Here they celebrate triumphs and allow every triumph, no matter how big or how small, to matter. These people are star-gazers.

RECOLLECTIONS

MEMORIES OF ARVON

Penelope Shuttle

How often have I wished that my memory was as good as that of my late Dad, who into his eighties could still recall the names of the pre-war Brentwood football team at the first game his own father took him to in 1924. But for me my own past is a strange and cobwebby place shot through with bright gleams, with oases of clear memory among the deserts of forgetting.

One such oasis takes me back to the summer of 1970 or 71, when Peter Redgrove ran a writing course, with co-tutor Anthony Thwaite, at the Beaford Centre in Devon. This was Arvon before Totleigh Barton. I was 23 years old, along for the ride, not yet having the experience or confidence to be a tutor. The course participants stayed in local B&Bs. I remember The Orchard Players rehearsing in the room next door.

It was here at The Beaford Centre that I met John Moat, a tall, rangy man, brimming with enthusiasm for what would become Arvon. He was kind, welcoming, full of gentle humour and a tangible love of poetry. Peter and I continued to meet John over the years, and to exchange volumes of our poetry.

In later years Peter and I tutored together at Totleigh, and my memories of John are woven in with recollections of times there. I recall one evening when Ted Hughes was guest reader. The Barn had not been converted then, and everyone squeezed into the sitting room. Ted gave a wonderful generous reading, and there was a festive gathering afterwards, John was there, of course, and, I think, Paul Roche...

I also have fond memories of early days at Totleigh when the group would go down to the village shop in Sheepwash to buy the makings for the evening meals, which were often surprising and inventive. It was always a joy to go over to Julia's office, where she had immediate answers to every query, solutions to any problem...

In the early days when Totleigh Barton was the sole Arvon centre it was still inventing itself. It has now, of course, branched out far and wide into the Arvon we now have. The template of the Arvon course, created by John Moat and John Fairfax, his co-founder – morning workshops, writing afternoons, one to one tutorials, shared cooking and communal meals, evening readings, and the tutors always on hand to talk to participants – has proved to be the ideal and workable pattern of how a course should be.

The Arvon template is now widely followed in centres in UK and Europe, acknowledged to be the best of all ways to bring budding, developing and published writers together to share and critique and celebrate writing. Countless participants have been given permission to claim identity as a writer because of Arvon, and many friendships have been forged.

To step over the threshold into Totleigh Barton has always been to step into a real world of writing and experience that is a birthright world for writers and readers but which the hard facts of daily life prevent all of us from accessing fully, so our times at Arvon are immeasurably valuable.

Writers in all genres owe a huge debt to 'the two Johns' and their vision and realisation of Arvon. My own writing life would have been the poorer without it, and my memories, patchy and adrift as they are, continue to surprise me with sudden recovered Arvon hours and events, often shared with Peter Redgrove, so that Arvon is an essential part in the tapestry of our life together.

To create a place where Imagination and language are so valued and put at the heart of life is Arvon's great achievement. These magical qualities, the open doors of Arvon, have added greatly to the strength of the writing community. Just imagine if Arvon had never happened!

Thank you, John!

The poem I have chosen is an extract from 'A Taliesin Answer' by Peter Redgrove. He often used the myth of Taliesin, the shape-shifter, in his writing workshops at Totleigh Barton.

What have you been?
A thunderharvest of twinkling grain.
A vivid gang of molten pig-iron.
The great man-eating skull that opens against the sky.
A whistle made from the wingbone of an eagle.

What have you been?
Escape from murder in the posthole.
A door opening on a stairway.
Frankensputin's monster.
The great luminous brain.

What have you been?
A nice meat pie without cartilage.

A wound in air.
The path of least resistance through the water.
The great Christmas reefer passed hand to hand along Hadrian's Wall.
The hiss of thick slices of bacon.

What have you been?
The loose shawl of a minister in the wood sitting alone on a log.
The subfusc overalls of a lawyer of note: much heated mud is flying.
A ladder of smoke on which a spirit climbs to heaven; I pass away.

What have you been?
A rain-begetter, a rain-splitter,
I had twenty-three aluminium eyes and long red hair like a horse's tail.
I was a frail sea-ear, a shell in the Atlantic fetch, listening;
An octagonal correspondence;
A leech daily regaled on the white rump of a lady of quality....

FIVE DAYS

MAGGIE GEE

The first evening: it's Monday already! People are arriving in ones and bunches down long lanes, dragging bags to upstairs bedrooms, looking shyly and at angles at each other or talking too fast at dinner; and then the expectant silence, tautened by a little fear, in the big room with the shadows behind them and an owl outside as they wait to see what the tutors might ask them to do before bedtime. Then quite suddenly it takes form, something like a game, perhaps, something that frees the pen or the voice inside, and everyone is quiet, a few look round the walls for help, then heads go down, there's a low rustling, yes they're writing, the spirit is in the room… It has begun.

Why do I feel a sense of freedom on the Monday I arrive, even though I still get a little nervous, and I know what follows will be one of the hardest-working weeks of my year? As creative writing courses pop up all over the land, spreading from universities to publishers, agencies and newspapers, what still makes Arvon special? Why is Arvon still a breath of green air – that name with an echo of 'Arden' about it, a promise of something joyful and Arcadian as well as lots and lots of new words?

Arvon is not academic. It produces no qualification, it offers no credits to eager American students abroad, it speaks not of theory, it does not grade. It isn't an industry marriage bureau, introducing tense beginners to a shiny array of publishing insiders (though people do fall in love and in friendship here – unsurprisingly, for they tend to feel happy and free.) It isn't formulaic, though the old original pattern mostly survives: the morning classes, the afternoons to wander and write, the final evening performance and the one-on-ones with the two tutors – I can't say "with the two writers," because at Arvon, everyone is a writer: for five or six days we are all touched with magic dust as the ordinary world where people might be software engineers or teachers or mothers or postmen or therapists, slips away. Arvon is not functional (though it is practical) and it is not unaffordable: as creative writing courses become more and more expensive, the near-week at Arvon remains, to my mind, the best value of all. It is not a con, and it is not taught by people whose only qualification is that they themselves have done a creative writing MA; here writers teach writers (John Moat said that "with any art or craft it is only the living and practice of it that provides the authority that can offer someone else genuine guidance.")

What is Arvon, then? It's a haven, and a bit of heaven. A place where no one need be embarrassed to love words or books, or by wanting very much to write better. A place of equality, where everyone except the tutors (who are probably reading new work) cooks and washes up and sets the tables, and where the enjoyment of the food and, often wine, increases as the pace of work builds up and the need to relax for a while and like each other grows. A place where teachers and students live together and share laughs, and where lots of the talk about writing doesn't happen in class. A place where days are longer and there are no TVs or boxed sets of DVDs to eat up the evening. A simpler place, where the plainness of the rooms implies that money doesn't matter. By contrast, the glory of the countryside outside the window – whether you are in The Hurst with its high sloping garden and loping hilltop walks, or Totleigh Barton with its low water-meadows and lowing cows, or Lumb Bank with its long sunset views across the valley to the blue-green woods beyond, or Moniack Mhor with its radiant northern bleakness and sense that the sun will skim the horizon and never go down – the countryside is waiting for you all year round, for the land and the air are free, an extra that comes with the course, a perilous and gorgeous incitement to walks and poems.

What are my personal memories? Not the 'star' students, though at least half a dozen of the writers I have taught at Arvon have gone on to be published, often years later, and that has always been a thrill – for the interest does not die on the day the tutor, by now exhausted, hauls her large case to the yard where the taxi will send her whizzing back to the train. Yes, Pat Barker was taught here by Angela Carter, and Lesley Glaister by Hilary Mantel: still that is not what Arvon promises, or what makes it special.

I know it in my bones, but now I have to try and analyse it too. This is what I think. Writing here is at once a spiritual practice, a value, and a place of deep refuge; a way of understanding one's life and communicating it to others who will listen; and a focus of concentrated 'craft' work, something that has to be enacted in the detail of every sentence written. It is a process of becoming, and becoming more free. Now I shall look at what John Moat said, because he and John Fairfax, the only begetters of it all, should know, and this is what he says, and I'm not too far off: "the capacity to be open and responsive to the Imagination is every child's, every individual's most precious gift. When that gift is realised, i.e. when the individual has thus uniquely expressed him or herself, then this is the unique gift that each has to offer." In my experience, writing is also a source of many confessions and uproarious laughter: everyone has been unfaithful to the Muse in one way or another, everyone has failed or been blocked, everyone has found words hard even as their love for them increased, and here it is all right to admit to it all in the knowledge that the others understand, and want to know. Here is a place where you do not have to justify yourself: writing is a way of being more alive.

I remember getting very tired in the early days of Arvon teaching when I didn't realise that it isn't feasible to read the 10,000 words of novel that a student happens to have brought with him and hopes you will have read by breakfast, because unless you sleep, you won't be on form for the morning class. Soon I started to understand I must pace myself, read a few pages very carefully rather than too many pages superficially, and always make time to have a walk in the beautiful countryside before supper. I learned to trust in the Arvon alchemy that means – so far, touch wood – that by the last evening there will be a radiant glow of goodwill and fellow-feeling around for the final performance, and that even the writers who were most frightened when they first had to read out to fifteen strangers will have relaxed, and will be giving the reading their all. I have learned to trust that the evening meals, though perhaps Tuesday's seems to pose a near-insuperable challenge to people who have never cooked for eighteen before, will have turned by Friday into a flamboyant celebration, with each set of cooks trying to outdo the one before in their desire to celebrate something beautiful, transient and real: the love that mysteriously starts to envelope the group as the week goes on. "Feel the love" is a phrase that always seems to hover over the final evening at Arvon, and if that sounds completely over the top, I am guessing that you've never been on an Arvon course.

I have been on a course as a student too, in Totleigh Barton two years ago, where I learned about writing plays from playwright Nell Leyshon and producer and theatre manager Frances Poet. I discovered just how precarious it can seem when you are reading out very new, unedited work, but also how Arvon starts you writing new things, gives you new perspectives, intensively teaches techniques you don't know, takes you out of your comfort zone but also consoles you with new friendships, new people, new skills, new sources of pleasure. I haven't actually managed to write an entire play yet, but I have begun writing, and have publicly performed, dramatic monologues, and find that my novel-in-progress is also pushing its way to life in a territory new to me, halfway between a book and a play. Slowly but surely, the Arvon alchemy is transforming something in my work, as I have seen it do for others so many times. It is what I wanted and needed: I asked and I was fed, not just by the wonderful Nell and Frances but by my fellow students – thank you, friends.

Now I must say thank you to Arvon – and marvel. In this strange British Isles of ours, in many ways a world that has narrowed and darkened since the 1960s, Arvon has stayed unchanged and yet youthful. It has not become over-groomed, not spawned a nervous series of new mission statements, not professionalised and privatised itself into sterility. It is basically four houses in the country through which a pilgrim's progress of human beings passes, staying a while to write and to share their writing, with good helpers, and good company. Thank you John Fairfax and John Moat for what you give again and again through your faith in the Imagination, beginning as you did "like a couple of sorcerer's apprentices," as John Moat says, "watching in amazement as the spell constantly came up with the goods."

And now it is the final evening; it's Friday, so soon! And the long dark table has been decorated with wild blossom in bottles and vases and the white petals are lit by candles in saucers, and in the background an open fire is burning, cheeks are flushed and people are holding back a little on the wine because soon it will happen, the thing itself, the performance, the finale, and the conversation flows bright and deep over small disruptions of laughter until everything is eaten and the dishes are washed and we troop across to the barn again where it all started, and silence falls as the MC introduces the first writer, and the new words sound in the high cave that holds us, and we listen to the best of what we have found and made, ending with another beginning, the only way to end. It's happening again as it has done for decades, the enactment of John Moat's great and generous vision of new writing, newly shared: "Here is the intention: to arrive at the beginning and to know the place for the first time. Omega, the ultimate coming home. Alpha and Omega,— the beginning and the end of the Story."

MY LIFE AT TOTLEIGH BARTON

MONIQUE ROFFEY

IN THE SPRING of 1999, a woman called Julia Wheadon agreed to give me a bursary to attend a writing workshop that summer at a house called Totleigh Barton in Devon. The workshop would be tutored by two writers: Andrew Miller and Emily Perkins – I hadn't heard of either of them. Immediately I went out and bought their books *Ingenious Pain* and *Not Her Real Name*. I was thirty-four years old – just back from a year teaching English in East Jerusalem. I was volunteering for Amnesty International. I'd been attending a regular writing group in London and working on short stories and I was taken up with the idea that I would one day be a published author. Someone told me about Arvon and I ordered a brochure. I was excited to be going on a week-long residential course in the countryside. A Londoner, I rarely ventured beyond Zone 2. I was broke and the bursary meant I could attend a course that I couldn't really afford. I packed a small bag and pens and notebooks (I'm not sure if laptops even existed then) and took a train down to Exeter to visit a friend near the writing centre. On the Monday afternoon the course was to begin, my friend drove me into the pebbly courtyard of Totleigh Barton, between the large saffron coloured cob barn and the converted pigsties which were to be our rooms.

That was thirteen years ago. For me, the week was life changing.

Somewhere I still have the copy of *Ingenious Pain* Andrew Miller signed on the Friday the course ended. I was going to do an MA in Creative Writing at Lancaster University that September, where he'd done his PhD and written *Ingenious Pain* under the supervision of the infamous David Craig. In this copy I have stuffed some part of a writing exercise he set us that week – and also contributed to. I have a sample of his handwriting on some paper in a book he wrote which he signed too, a book he wrote at the same university where I was going to study to be a writer. It was all significant. Andrew was all cheekbones and mischievous flashing eyes; I nursed a small crush on him for a week. I gave him and Emily a few pages of cramped awful bits of writing, but by the end of the week thawed-out enough to slip some pages of erotic writing under the door of Andrew's room – which had been an old goose hut. He liked it! Andrew Miller, one of the finest contemporary writers around, liked my work. Wow. We sat at a picnic table in the garden at Totleigh Barton and even told me as much. Little did I know, then, that one day I would sit to write an erotic memoir in my mid-forties. Those early pages Andrew saw were the first scratchings of a fledgling author who would go on to explore and write about her sexual life.

On that course I met two fellow students who were to become friends, the writers Donna Daley-Clarke and Emily Pedder. We soon set up a small London-based writing group at my flat in Shepherd's Bush and met a few times that summer to discuss our work. That first week as a student of Arvon, working with Andrew Miller and Emily Perkins, meeting other aspiring writers, gave me a taste of what I could be, how my life could pan out if I worked hard. It gave me a small peer group to know and work with, a tiny cadre of apprentice authors, my first ever writer chums. Crucially, that week also gave me my first experience of self-identification as an author. Before that course I didn't know exactly what an author was.

Authors are hidden to us. They are embedded in society, secret, a community of one in every town all over the world. They work alone, they don't really have colleagues; while they do have an editor, this editor isn't really a boss. I'd never spotted a real-life author before, only seen names on books: Dickens, Atwood, Vonnegut. What did an apprentice author look like? What did authors wear to work? How and where did they work? During that week I came to realise that authors were inward, bookish types who took care to write things down, usually because they had a love of language and also because they felt the urge to create stories from fantasy and reality on the page. I came away realising that I looked just like everyone else on the course, or rather, I recognised myself in them. If they were writers, so was I. This, though weird and perhaps even naive, was a revelation.

A couple of months later, September 1999, I went off to do my MA at Lancaster University and began my first novel *sun dog*. There, I also met my teacher and first mentor Linda Anderson, my first agent Simon Trewin and my (now ex-) partner of six years, fellow writer Ian Marchant. These were early but pivotal years. I was writing my first novel, meeting other writers, living with a writer, becoming a writer and then Linda Anderson, head of the MA at Lancaster, put me up for a mentoring scheme run by Arvon in partnership with the Jerwood Foundation, which I was lucky enough to secure. Then, as part of the prize, I was sent back to Totleigh Barton for a hothouse week of one-to-one mentoring. Here, I met my second mentor, the writer Richard Beard. Together, we spent days discussing my next novel, a story about a ghost and an old spinster who shared a house on an unenclosed heath south of Croydon. This was to be my second novel, *Removed*. Like Andrew Miller, Richard Beard was dashing and clever and writerly, and had written a few novels. I thought he was smashing; like Andrew, Richard became a friend. By then I was beginning to piece together who and what authors were and looked like (handsome) and what they did (write a lot).

It was over dinner one night that week, in December 2001, around the enormous oaken banquet table in the dining hall at Totleigh Barton, that I overheard Andy Brown, then Centre Director, say to Richard Beard that he and his then partner Amy Shelton had quit their post after six years. Arvon would be advertising their posts in the New Year, 2002. My ears pricked up – jobs? Running this magnificent old house? Already I had developed 'feelings' for the old house; there was something about its foot thick snug walls, the padding of the thatched roof, the massive oak beams above the fireplace that had made me feel secure, cosseted in those two weeks I had been a student. Totleigh Barton was made of mud, which is more or less what cob is. Its beams had been sawn from the forests all around, the thatch was once taken from the Somerset Levels. The old house was a masterwork of organic architecture, somehow thrust up from the very ground it stood on. It was a quiet humble home, self assured and comfortable.

Totleigh Barton also possessed enormous charisma, a personality of its own. Of course, I'd heard stories of a ghost – a young servant girl who'd once lived in the tiny room next to the stairs (now a broom cupboard). Of course, I'd also heard of John Moat, his wife Antoinette and John Fairfax, the founders and some of the stories about Arvon's early days. But could we run this house for writers, should we apply? We were two penniless near-starving writers, housed in an infamous co-op in north London. Would Arvon have us?

My then partner Ian Marchant was six foot three, bald, snaggle-toothed and pigeon-toed. When he laughed, which was often, a boom erupted from his chest; he was luvvy-ish and prone to making rather blue jokes. He wore very thick-lensed black Eric Morecambe-style spectacles and old suits which stank of mothballs. He was well-read, raffish, working class, and was not just an author but one half of a ramshackle and anarchic light entertainment duo *Your Dad*. When I got home from that week I told him that a job was going. He'd visited Totleigh too as a student and knew the house. We ummed and ahhed, but knew that really we must decide to apply for the joint job as Centre Directors – it would be an incredible adventure. It took us a week of creative arguing – but nevertheless we managed to put an application in the post.

Amazingly, weeks later, we were short-listed. When we went for the interview at Totleigh Barton in February 2002, I knew they would size us up – and it would either be a 'yes' or a 'no.' We had rehearsed a good cop/bad cop routine, (me being the bad cop). Ian fluttered his eyelids and *ooh*ed and *ahh*ed and made literary asides. We took it in turns to answer questions. Ian wore a charcoal black suit and we polished his head so it glowed like a baby's bum. I wore an olive green batwing knitted top, tweed slacks and red clogs. Cello, the ancient and proprietorial tabby cat, jumped on my lap mid-interview – *you're in*, she whispered. Of course they loved us. She's nice and bossy, they thought, will get things done. He's unique, a one-off.

And so, in May 2002, we moved to Sheepwash, Devon in our old green and white striped 2CV Dolly, crammed with bags; behind us followed two Luton vans full of our belongings, one of these vans containing only books. We were to take up posts as Centre Directors of Totleigh Barton. For the next four years we would be custodians of a grand old cob manor house, we were to be the thirteenth pair of Directors to be appointed to the job.

I made that journey to Totleigh Barton with Ian Marchant ten years ago. Quickly, it had happened. I had become a writer; *sun dog* was soon to be published. It was three years since Andrew Miller had read my work on the picnic bench in Totleigh's back garden. I hadn't yet met John

Moat or his wife Antoinette, or John Fairfax, the legendary founders of Arvon. Ted Hughes was dead, *Birthday Letters*, a huge success. The newest and third Arvon centre, The Hurst, was under construction. We arrived in convoy one spring evening, into the square at Sheepwash, hopeful and fresh. We were starting a new life.

We met John Moat fairly early on, in June 2002. Luckily, he was scheduled to tutor with Lindsay Clarke in our very first open course programme. The Wednesday night he read in the barn, I remember sitting on the floor, not too far from the leather chair he sat in. I wanted to drink him in, learn from him. Through setting up Arvon, John Moat had already given me so much: a sense of self as an author, a handful of writer chums, a working mentor (Richard Beard) – and now a job. I was new at this job, but already it had been dawning on me just how important Arvon was to the literary culture of the country. Already I had been meeting tutors, heard them tell their Arvon stories; already I had an understanding that Arvon had fostered numerous connections like the ones I had already made myself and had been doing so for decades. Arvon had not just been breeding aspiring writers, such as myself, but more importantly, had been knitting together a culture of co-operation and generosity of spirit amongst these loner-writers who, without Arvon, might never know or meet each other. Arvon was giving these loner-writers a sense of community, was pulling together a school of like-minded spirits committed to the pen.

That night, ten years ago, the John Moat I met was shy, polite, friendly, gallant. His eyes were turquoise and fiery. His cheeks were pink, his silver hair rather long and flopped over his forehead. He was handsome! And he was unassuming – and his face crinkled with aliveness and mirth. He was a poet and he had much to say about poetry and writing and yet I had a sense that he was full of secrets, his own feelings about life, and many more poems to write. He was a man quite clearly taken up with the same vocation I was – to write and lead a writer's life.

I met him many times after that, along with his wife Antoinette. Frequently one or both of them would drop by. Sometimes they came on the weekend and brought a picnic; sometimes they came and had lunch with us and the tutors on a Friday lunchtime. Frequently they invited us for Sunday lunch. We went for walks with them around Welcombe, they took an interest in who we were and how things were doing, but in terms of running the centre, they hung back. Once, I do remember there was an issue around signage in the centre for health and safety reasons. John flew into a tizzy. The standard issue plastic heath and safety signs were ugly, he said – and he was right. He set about making health and safety signs which would be kinder on the eye and suit the house. He arrived with his own hand-penned signs, writ in gold ink on black card in his famous bubble-style italics.

It is impossible to describe those four years I spent as custodian at Totleigh Barton without passion. It is hard to know what to speak about most, what was the best part, the most fun, the most inspiring, how to talk about what I learnt. All those people we met! There are countless moments which spring to mind: listening to students read their work in the barn, watching over them in the kitchen as they put together a meal for twenty, welcoming in a new group on a Monday night. Then there was the love affair with the house, the house martins in the eaves above the kitchen door, the frisky and inquisitive bullocks in the fields, the tinkly River Torridge, Julia Wheadon, Noel and his huge hound Timmy. While we were on watch no one died and the house didn't catch fire. Those were my two biggest worries. I'm proud of that. While we were there, the house was clean and the sheets were laundered and there was lots of wine and food on the table. We kept the house warm in winter and we grew tomatoes in summer. While we were there, the water table lowered and the well ran dry. We had to get diviners in to dig a new well. Also, the old Ford estate died. The two tabby cats, born at Totleigh, also died, first Stripy and then Cello. Ian buried them both under a tree by the pond. While we were there Mimi Khalvati gave me the only first hand witness account of the ghost. She'd once seen her, in broad daylight, the ghost of a young girl out by the pond. She saw Mimi seeing her and slipped away through the gate, back through Totleigh's front door. Mimi wrote a poem about this young girl and you can find this poem in a collection by Mimi Khalvati in Totleigh's poetry library.

I could go on and on but I won't. I left Totleigh Barton as Centre Director six years ago and have since returned numerous times as an Arvon tutor. Arvon is remarkable. Not only did it give me an identity as a writer and a satisfying job, but over the last dozen years or so it has given me a family, a place, Totleigh Barton, which I call a home. It is one of several places on earth I call home, but nevertheless, Totleigh is one of them. Arvon has given me a community of fellow authors to know and call on.

Arvon has cultivated the literary talents and ambitions of hundreds of writers in the UK for two generations now. It has fostered countless lineages of talent. I know for a fact that Andrew Miller was tutored by Angela Carter at Totleigh Barton at the age of eighteen. And Andrew Miller in turn tutored and inspired me. I know that Carol Ann Duffy discovered Kate Clanchy on an Arvon course, that Neil Rollinson worked with Peter Redbridge, that Andy Brown worked with John Burnside – and so on. Hundreds of poets and writers have encouraged each other and formed themselves because of Arvon; thousands of people have met at Totleigh and other Arvon centres across the country. Thousands of poems have been written at Totleigh. There is much made of the notion of "Arvon magic," and when I think of this I remember John Moat in that leather armchair the first time I met him in the barn, a poet, those crinkly turquoise eyes, alive with mirth – and with secrets. A magician? Yes. Quite simply Arvon has magic – why wouldn't it? – it was founded by magicians.

A HAND OF FRIENDSHIP AND A HEART OF LOVE

Satish Kumar

I FIRST MET John Moat in 1978 when I was living with my family in Wales on a farm set in the woods of the Preselli hills. One morning John Lane and John Moat came down the long drive in search of *Resurgence* magazine, which promotes self-sufficiency, organic farming, rural crafts and simple living. They were researching projects, programmes and activities concerned with living sustainably on the land. At the time, both of them were engaged in establishing the Yarner Trust in South and North Devon, where young people could be given knowledge, experience and training in self-sufficiency. Antoinette, John's wife had donated an eleventh century farmhouse, Welcombe Barton, together with six acres of land for this purpose.

"With your Gandhian background and connections with E F Schumacher and his philosophy of Small Is Beautiful, can you tell us what would be the best way to establish a centre for self-sufficiency?" asked John Moat.

"Ideas have power when they can be embodied by people of conviction and commitment," I said. "So, you have to find people for whom self-sufficiency is not just an idea but a way of life."

During this conversation I discovered that John Moat was not only an idealist for rural life and self-sufficiency, but also a poet, a novelist, a painter and a man with a great sense of humour. Having been the editor of *Resurgence* for five years at that time, I felt that the thing missing from the magazine was humour, and so, during that very first meeting, I asked John if we would consider writing a humorous column for *Resurgence*.

"It's very good of you to ask," said John, with his characteristic humility. "Let me think about it – I'll be in touch."

I walked with my new – and as it turned out to be, life-long – friends around the farm, showing them the vegetable garden and introducing them to our goats and cows. They could sense the spirit of joy in self-sufficiency and that encouraged them to found the Yarner Trust in Devon.

From the very start, our relationship was both literary and practical. As it turned out, for various reasons, our stay in West Wales was destined to be only temporary.

"Actually, we're looking for a place that can become our permanent home," I told them. "One where we can continue to publish *Resurgence* and live close to the land."

"Would you consider coming to live in Devon?" asked John.

"Why not?" I replied. "All options are open." Although we were meeting for the first time, it was as if we had known each other for ever.

As soon as John Moat got back home to North Devon, not only did he write to us to thank us for our hospitality but he sent me the first of what was to be his regular column, which he called *Didymus* – otherwise know as Doubting Thomas. It was an extremely erudite and very amusing piece – I did not need to edit or change a single word, and it was published in the September/October issue of *Resurgence* in 1978. Between 1978 and 2011 we have published 100 *Didymus* columns.

Every time I receive *Didymus* typed on John's old typewriter with some handwritten corrections, I feel a sense of delight – it just makes me smile. He combines satire and humour with profound spirituality, deep politics and always a fresh approach to the subject in hand. Subtle, never repetitive and ever punctual, John really is an editor's dream writer. There are many regular contributors to *Resurgence* but no one else has made it to 100 contributions! His column has been the glue to our friendship for thirty-four years.

As a further indication of the friendship we were to enjoy, not only did John join the ranks of *Resurgence* but he, with Antoinette, started looking in his local vicinity for a house with land for my wife June and I, and our two young children, Mukti and Maya. By May 1979 they found Ford House just on the outskirts of Hartland, which was to be auctioned within a few days of my seeing it. As this was my first ever experience of a public auction to buy a house, I was extremely nervous, so John and Antoinette accompanied me. John sat on my left and Antoinette on my right.

"Keep bidding until you get it!" John instructed me. He was as keen for me to have the house as I was, and with growing excitement, I continued to bid until we did indeed get it! We were to become neighbours of seven miles distance – but that was no distance at all to our friendship. We moved in at the end of July 1979 to find freshly-baked bread and a bottle of red wine waiting to welcome us. Not only had John and Antoinette found us the house and come to the auction to support me, but they generously contributed towards the repair and renewal of the house so that we should be comfortable and happy in our new home.

John's generosity never made us feel we were under any obligation and this is how John works: not only towards us but to a large number of writers, poets, teachers, artists, editors and activists to whom, over the years, he has lent a hand of friendship and a heart of love.

John is a poet, a painter and a novelist, but he is not cut off from the real world. He is engaged in the renewal of rural arts and crafts as well as being a committed peace activist. His quiet support to numerous peace organisations complements his many artistic pursuits. One afternoon John and Antoinette rang me to say they had an idea that they would like to discuss with me, so could they invite themselves to Ford House for a cup of tea?

"Of course," I said. "I am here – come at any time." Within half an hour there was a knock at the door.

"That was quick!" I knew there must be some urgency to their plans.

As I was pouring tea, John said, "We have been talking about the appalling state of militarism around the world – so many peace movements, so many demonstrations, so much peace literature – but nothing seems to make any difference. Perhaps we need a more subtle approach?"

"What do you have in mind?" I asked.

"Something more like homeopathy, such as the power of positive thinking – the power of prayer, if you like," said John.

"It has to be a universal prayer, a prayer which transcends religious divisions, a prayer which anybody and everybody can say – whether they are people of faith or no faith," I suggested.

"Yes, of course," said John. "That's what we mean and that's what we want to achieve. It's what humanity needs! Antoinette's original idea was a prayer that can be said around the world; that can be translated into any language."

We agreed to try and find something suitable. I kept thinking all afternoon and all evening – I was intrigued by the idea. That night, in bed, I suddenly remembered three lines of a prayer from the Upanishads.

I got up and wrote them down – a free translation from Sanskrit with a few additional lines.

Next morning I read the words to John and Antoinette over the phone. They liked the composition, wrote it down and came to us later that morning with some refinements to the text. John named it the Universal Peace Prayer and later it became known as the Prayer for Peace.

> Lead me from death to life
> From falsehood to truth;
> Lead me from despair to hope
> From fear to trust;
> Lead me from hate to love
> From war to peace.
> Let peace fill our hearts
> Our world, our universe.
> Peace, peace, peace.

With John and Antoinette's complete commitment and dedication the Prayer for Peace spread around the world in many languages. It was said in the Kremlin in the presence of Mikhail Gorbachev and in 10 Downing Street in the presence of Margaret Thatcher. The campaign was masterminded from St James's Church, Piccadilly, after it was publically launched by Mother Teresa of Calcutta.

"Every day at noon, put your positive vibrations towards peace by saying this prayer," urged Mother Teresa. This was a very foresightful idea as somewhere in the world at every moment, it is midday, so the Prayer for Peace was being constantly chanted all around the world, like a chain of contemplation.

Who knows what effect it has had? But it certainly created a new consciousness among various political, religious and cultural leaders. This is one example of John's activism – there are many others.

On a personal note, it has been a great source of joy for my wife June and me to live in close proximity to John and Antoinette. John is a man for all seasons: every spring there would be a call.

"Satish! The magnolia's blooming magnificently! Come and see." John would say.

Of course, we would eagerly go. Before we sat down under the magnolia for our cup of tea, we would enjoy a walk through the bluebells and primroses in the oak wood behind their house above the vegetable garden. Lost in the blue haze of Crenham Mill and under the spell of the sweet smell of spring, we knew ourselves fortunate to have the friendship of the magical Moats.

After our walk around the gardens, we would sit down under the magnolia tree, often blessed by the warm sun, enjoying a cup of tea and good conversation. Writing, painting and activism combined with spontaneous celebration of life's bounteous gifts is John's recipe for a good life.

We'd usually have another call in the summer.

"The garden's full of the scent of roses. Do come for a cup of tea," John would say, and who could resist? We go.

Before we see the roses, we wander around the vegetable garden to see the onions, the garlic, peas, beans and lettuces. John's vegetable garden is no less abundant than his flower garden. We enjoy both. Red, pink and white roses are only the bait – John and Antoinette take us through clematis, phlox, irises, water lilies in the pond and even the last of the wisteria. What a privilege it is to celebrate summer together.

Our autumn invitation is slightly different. At this time, in addition to ourselves, a number of other friends are invited to visit the Peace

Grove where twenty-five oak trees were planted on the 'eleventh hour of the eleventh day of the eleventh month' in 1998. John offered a home for the oak trees that were given to me in celebration of my twenty-five years editing *Resurgence*. We say the Prayer for Peace in honour of all those who gave their lives for peace, in the world's wars. We stand among the bracken and listen to the sound of the sea on the other side of the hill. After some moments of contemplation we make our way back to Crenham Mill for steaming soup, bread and cheese and the easy conversation of friends, admiring John's plaits of giant onions – prize-winners in the village show – draped side-by-side with his vibrant paintings of summer flowers.

And so we come to winter – at John's home, a time for mulled wine by the fire in the living room, decorated with great lengths of ivy, holly and a Christmas tree. We are invited to participate in a farewell to the old year and a welcome to the new. We sit sipping warmed wine, reading aloud poems and passages which inspire and enlighten: John reads from *Zen Mind, Beginner's Mind* or *Cutting Through Spiritual Materialism* by Chogyam Trungpa, one of his favourite writers.

Once, John came by some 300-year-old, exceptionally beautiful Tibetan handmade paper, which he sent to Chogyam Trungpa. Lo and behold, one sheet was returned with amazingly robust calligraphy by Trungpa himself, that now hangs in John's living room, together with Shakti the Hindu goddess of power in the lap of Lord Shiva, the god of love, fertility and dissolution. In John and Antoinette's home, these Buddhist and Hindu icons sit comfortably with Christian angels, kneeling as they hold candles symbolising the light within and without.

We join in with our own readings: Antoinette reads a passage by Lama Govinda; June from Thich Nhat Hanh and I from Rabindranath Tagore. At 11.30pm John reaches for the faggot of wood that he has collected during the day and bound. It contains twigs of oak and ash, holly and hawthorn, willow and ivy, beech and birch, alder and apple. The faggot is a perfect size to fit in the big woodburner. Watching the wood burn and blaze and crackle, we let burn all our fears, animosities, anxieties and anger. John and Antoinette have invited us, over many years, to witness this sacred ritual. By some miracle, exactly at midnight, the last twig of the faggot disappears into the glowing embers and we toast the New Year.

John Moat is a many-faceted man. A Renaissance man, a cook, gardener, poet, painter, engraver, teacher, activist, mentor and much, much more. He is like a medieval alchemist, constantly experimenting to turn the ordinary into the extraordinary. He can turn base matter into gold.

ARVON AND EDUCATION

TED HUGHES

This essay first appeared as the Foreword to The Way to Write *by John Fairfax and John Moat (Penguin Books, 1998), and is reprinted here by kind permission of Carol Hughes. It remains in the copyright of The Estate of Ted Hughes.*

THESE CHAPTERS HAVE grown naturally out of the work the authors have done with apprentice writers on the courses given by Arvon, over the last twelve years.

Since Arvon provides the living context of almost everything they have to say, perhaps it would be as well to start by explaining a little of what it is and how it began. John Moat and John Fairfax, the two authors of this book, invented it. They had come to feel (like many another) that the conventional methods of teaching English are unsatisfactory and, except where they are adapted by some exceptional teacher, fail to give students any guidance in the art of writing well, or any real idea of what makes creative language live, of how literature is made and why it is important, or of the fact that it is students who grow eventually into the people who produce all these books. John Moat and John Fairfax felt they knew what was wrong, and it seemed to them they knew how to correct it. Twelve years ago, all they asked for was a group of students who wanted to learn about writing. So they got them. They put their faith to the practical test, and organised a five-day course.

Their idea was simple. It was: to gather about fourteen young people who were interested enough to make the effort, and two writers, in a secluded house, where all would live together for five days, working at writing. The only 'instruction' given would be what rose directly out of that involvement – the apprentice working, and the master guiding him as he worked, showing him how to work, helping him to work.

There is a Japanese proverb: "Don't study an art, practice it." And Sir Francis Bacon wrote: "Example is a globe of precepts." And these were the main working principles: practice from the apprentice, example from the master; that was all there was to it, plus the five-day concentration on a common purpose, and seclusion.

John Fairfax and John Moat tutored the first course themselves. The students all came from mid-Devon and only one or two of them had made any attempt to write 'creatively' before. As it happened, I looked in on that launching of what was to become The Arvon Foundation, and for several reasons I was made to remember it.

Some months before, John Moat had visited me and outlined his plan, hoping that I would be interested and perhaps agree to be a tutor on one of the proposed courses. I daresay my reaction dismayed him, because as I recall I told him more or less outright that I thought the scheme was unworkable. It was the first time we had met. I think if I had known better what an unusual character I was listening to, I would have answered less definitely. Little did I suspect how dramatically my opinion of his idea was going to be reversed.

But at the time I simply felt he was wrong, and my negative was quite confident.

Before I say any more, I would like to dwell a little on that negative of mine, because it is not only mine. What exactly lay behind it? I have often had cause to ask myself this, because over the subsequent years, in my busy promotion of Arvon, I have again and again met that instant negative coming from others. Not a reasoned negative, but an automatic one – as if it crystallised, at a touch, out of a supersaturated solution.

What is particularly curious to me about my response, when I think of it now, is that I had quite strong reasons to say yes. Unlike many writers, I was a confirmed believer in 'poetic schools'. The notion of some modern version of the ancient Irish poetic schools, as evidence of them has come down to us, makes a deep appeal. That compulsory learning of a large body of traditional material, the incessant discipline in production, the methodical mobilising and training of every scrap of *potentia*, the nursing of artistic standards as sacred – at least – as athletic record performance: all that certainly grips the Imagination. And, however rudimentary, what John Moat proposed was surely the seed of something that might grow a branch that way, some day.

Also, I had seen one form of the 'master' and 'apprentice' relationship working successfully in the United States. At quite close quarters I watched Robert Lowell's writing classes transform Anne Sexton from a housewife who had written a few undistinguished lines but who wanted to learn how to write better, into a remarkable author able to express, overwhelmingly, all that she was. And I watched the same classes supervise crucial changes in Sylvia Plath's writing. Almost every young American writer I met had worked – in just that 'apprentice' role – with some chosen 'master'. Robert Lowell himself had sought out Crowe Ransom and Allen Tate – so determined that he even pitched his tent on Tate's lawn, and lived there. I had marvelled – not without some envy – at the range and energy and generosity, yes, and the seriousness of discussion between American writers and students. And I had felt the unselfconscious release of it, the charged positive atmosphere, the willingness to let the other man go his own way, the assumption that the greatest things are still to be done.

And what John Moat proposed surely pointed in the same direction.

My negative was so prompt, I think now, because I held a fixed, deeply sceptical preconception of what the English temperament would make of such an idea. And my first reference, for certain, was the usual English response to the idea of American Creative Writing classes. I had met it too often to doubt it. And that response is, almost inevitably, dismissive, and usually derisive too.

To go no further, to examine that reaction alone, leads immediately into a whole web of attitudes – commonly secreted but rarely interrogated – which all seem to share one decisive accent, and it is a negative accent: negative towards any deliberate cultivation of excellence, negative towards the methodical release of creative energy, negative towards enthusiasm, negative towards the future.

It would be an interesting exercise to search out the history and rise to power – even political power – of these attitudes, in our English life. It is a depressing exercise – but still interesting – to follow out their consequences, which amount to more than the amateurism and gentility, of which we so often accuse ourselves, though they supply some of the masks. Those attitudes do have real power: witness the plight of Education itself, which is the result of deliberate political decision. Education is a natural victim of the deadly negative, being the most essential of all our industries. With the most vital national product of all (future brains, abilities and skills to pull us out of the mess). It is interesting to see how these dominant attitudes have appropriated a show of the intellectual virtues, a large repertoire, with variants for each step of the social ladder. But the brightest show of mental alertness, and the heaviest show of moral righteousness (lightened by the much-admired inflection of irony) cannot conceal the fact that they are, in their fruits, negative, and are at bottom mechanical: the reflexes of a mass-hypnosis. Mass hypnosis is no doubt just one aspect of the unity of society, but in our case the mass-hypnosis is negative, so all the particles are negative. A mass-hypnosis can just as well be positive (the turn of the fifteenth/sixteenth centuries in England was certainly mass-hypnotised, but positively). In our case however, each one of us as a microcosm of our society, is afflicted with the negative sleep, in some degree or other, whether we like it or not, and each one of us has to struggle separately to become aware of it, and to awaken from it, in our own lives.

It was a strong sense of this web of our inertia that made me so sure about just what opposition John Moat's experiment would meet: opposition from the sources of the cash it would need, from the educational institutions that would have to co-operate to supply most of the students, and even from the students themselves.

These expectations of mine were sharply modified at my very next encounter with him. He had invited me to read verse to the students of that first course, on their last evening. And there for the first time I met what has since become familiar, the indescribable, strange, intense euphoria of a successful Arvon course. By the time I had looked through what these students had written in the previous five days, I was converted. Something extraordinary had happened. Somehow John Fairfax and John Moat had hit on a method that actually worked. The deep lanes of mid-Devon cast a dark, narrow shadow, but the voltage of new-found Imagination and eloquence and originality in these students' pages seemed like an explosion. I was taken by surprise and found myself immensely moved and excited.

It seemed to me that what had happened here was more intense than anything of the kind I had witnessed in the United States. It's an impression that has been often confirmed since, because, as is well known, that was only the first course of many. Arvon grew, till now it holds thirty courses a year in the Yorkshire centre at Lumb Bank and thirty at the original centre at Totleigh Barton in Devon, and over the years it has employed hundreds of writers as tutors. Evidently my feelings about the English temperament had overlooked something. That temperament – if such a common characteristic can be said to exist, without our terms being so general as to be meaningless – is apparently wonderfully well suited to Arvon. But then, maybe the American 'temperament' would respond to it just as intensely and passionately – and the Italian and the Chinese too for that matter – because it would be a new thing to all of them. The five day top-pressure, all-out concentration on producing, with writers and students, as masters and apprentices, living together, secluded from all outside interference, even doing their own cooking, is as far as I know unique to Arvon. And even if I am largely right about our prevailing mass-hypnosis (and published statistics say I am, they say we think we are on the whole in a phase of self-doubt and negative withdrawal, even if there were no other evidence), nevertheless the Arvon method has evidently hit on the precise formula, the perfect 'Open Sesame' needed to crack that shell of imposed national passivity-to-entropy, that simian laissez-faire, and release the original energy, the hidden creative energy, which is positive.

Still, we always have to answer the Questioner who sits so sly. And he asks: "So let us admit it is as you say, the Arvon course has this startling effect on the student for a few days, and he or she writes a page that astonishes him or her, and delights the tutors – but what then? Does the whole machinery of Arvon really come down to this: the student gazing in baffled joy at a few lines of writing, captured from that abnormal, euphoric few days – before it drops him back into the jaws of the world to be chewed up by the forces that chew up the rest of us?"

The answer is: Yes it does.

There is much more to that brief answer than might appear. It is too easy to underestimate the import of those few lines and that baffled joy. The moment has to be held under a microscope, and examined carefully. What exactly does happen there? It is too easy to dismiss it as an ephemeral event – an irrelevant and somewhat pathetic pause in the giant struggle of education towards responsibility and citizenship.

To feel the real significance of that seemingly miniature happening, we have to acknowledge what is perhaps not much acknowledged – that far-reaching inner changes, creative revelations of our inner self, the only part of us with any value, are usually triggered in the smallest fraction of time. The operations of the inner life are more analogous to microbiology than to the building of a motorway. Inevitably our lives are shaped by our daily work, but what transforms our innermost self – when it is transformed – are those momentary confrontations, either with some experience that somehow opens internal connections between unexplored parts of ourselves, or with some person whose mere presence, the mere example of their living being, does the same, or with some few seconds of spontaneous vision that does the same. The analogy is with contracting an infection – the single touch of the virus is enough, only in this case what spreads through the cells is illumination, a new richness of life, a deeper grip on ourselves.

And this does happen on Arvon courses. It cannot be measured, but we have the evidence of those students who describe an experience which can only be this, in some degree or other. And they are now very many.

Even so, it may be that the persistent Questioner will go on. "Is that enough?" he will ask. That hit-or-miss chance of starting somebody off on a new feeling about themselves, which might be illusory, which might lead them to dream up unreal futures for themselves, doomed to disappointment, which might even – horror! – fix them in a determination to become writers. Is that what Arvon is about? Do we really want more writers?

There is no arguing with one who lowers the meaning of everything by simply lowering the interpretation, and who distrusts all that is invisible and intangible. For one thing, he has all the hard evidence on his side, even when he goes on to tell us that man is a political animal: a machine only, and that all culture is an opiate, a temporary illusion, and that our inner lives are a vapour – of no more account or reality than the inner lives of slaughter-house sheep.

But by then we know we have to dismiss this Questioner much as we, respect his point of view. It is better, perhaps, not to let him get his teeth into the fact that those who have taken part in the stirring events of a good Arvon course are also sometimes troubled.

This troubled feeling is intimately blended with the exhilaration. It is a feeling somewhat akin to the near-despair a teacher sometimes feels – I have certainly felt it – confronting a class full of very bright eleven-year-olds. What sort of teaching can ever hope to take advantage of all that eager potential, all that joyful readiness to go to the limit?

When the Arvon student is put in possession of that creative self which was hitherto inaccessible, two things, in particular, suddenly become much more interesting: the working of language, and the use of literature. In other words, that event brings about, often in a very short time, but in an organic and natural way, what years of orthodox English teaching almost inevitably fail to bring about except in the most artificial and external way. The student is awakened to the real life of language, with all that implies of the physiology of words, their ancestry and history and dynamic behaviour in varying circumstances (of all abbreviated, in conventional teaching, under the heading: grammar). At the same time he is introduced to literature as a living organism, part of the human organism, something which embodies the psychological record of this drama of being alive, something which articulates and illuminates the depth and range and subtlety of being human. Literature becomes as personal to him as his own struggling abilities – no longer, as conventional teaching presents it (and can only present it), a museum of obsolete manners and dead artefacts, without any relevance to 'now and the future'.

And in all this, the student has not swallowed anything from outside. It has all been awakened inside. In the true sense of the word he has been 'educated'.

But this is not all. While this is happening, maybe the largest purpose of all is being achieved. Our best imaginative literature can well be called the sacred book of the tribe. It holds what we, as a tribe, have inwardly – and therefore with most decisive experience – lived through: it holds the inner vision we all share, the unbroken circle of our nationality. This living monument of our language is the closest thing we have to a mythology: it is sacred because it enshrines our deepest knowledge of ourselves as a people, the language-circuits of our thought and feeling. It holds the DNA of our consciousness as a spiritual unity. The literature and the language are one. And we value it for the same reason that all nations in good morale have valued their literature: it is the national soul we carry. And our intimate possession of it, and our attempt to relive and renew and develop its traditions in our own lives is what keeps us single and alive as a nation. And when a student has been awakened, as I have described, to language and literature, he has been initiated into custodianship of this sacred book, the coherence of Englishness. And if this is not important, I do not know what is. After all, it is very easy to let that inner coherence go. It is easy to reject or neglect our sacred book: all sorts of novelties can persuade a people to do that, and laziness, more surely than an invader's imposed law, can easily obliterate our continually renewed efforts to bind ourselves into it afresh. It is very easy for a nation to break up into fragments and die. It has often happened. And that misfortune is something that cannot be rationalised away.

So what is troubling about the success of the Arvon method is in that very success, the sight of these truly basic educational activities being so joyously grasped by the students – but for how long?

Any hope we might have for their survival, once the five days are over, must be qualified by what we know of the survival rate of natural talent, in contemporary England. One of the most suggestive arguments is to be found in the anthologies which have been published, for the last twenty-three years, by the annual Children's Literary Competition, run by WH Smith (it was formerly run by the *Daily Mirror*). In this Competition, between thirty thousand and sixty thousand entries are judged every year, from children all over the UK, in different age-groups between eight and seventeen-years-old. Each year, the judges of that Competition confront a display of natural verbal and imaginative gifts that could not easily be richer: what might be called maximum talent in this field seems to be not at all uncommon. But after twenty-three years, the judges are forced to ask: what has happened to them all? The impression is: they disappeared into some disintegrating gas, around the age of eighteen. Because almost without exception they have disappeared. The judges are forced to ask, too, whether the same nearly total wipe-out occurs in every other field, where the talent is less naturally visible.

The social epidemic, whatever it is, that swallows these, also waits for Arvon's students. We can accuse fashionable culture, which is certainly inimical to the nurture of language, and we can take the measure of that strange hostility to literature – to the written word in any form – which has even managed to acquire political status, and even a role in education, with an ideology and a revolutionary educational programme. And we can wonder about the tolerance where such hostility is called everything but high treason of a most effective sort. But these, after all, are only symptoms.

Which returns us forcibly to the motives behind this present book. During the twelve years of its existence, Arvon has exposed a large number of writers to the problems of being a course tutor. This steady effort of exploration and discovery, in the actual methods of working with apprentice writers, has accumulated gradually, as the tutors have returned again and again, sharing the work with fresh partners. It is this battery of experience which John Moat and John Fairfax have been able to tap. They have tutored regularly themselves, from that first course onwards, and as the originators of the whole idea they have come to feel, perhaps more acutely than anybody else, that the technical part of the work, at least, is something that ought to be shared more widely – among teachers, it may be, who have never heard of Arvon, and among students who will never get there.

Whatever happens on these courses – and as I have tried to indicate, much of what happens can be momentous in a psychological way – the actual hour-by-hour work is mainly a business of scrutinising language in action, a laborious business of discrimination and definition, fitting words to one precise purpose or another.

And this is an activity which can be exercised anywhere, in a classroom or in private. It does not need the special circumstances of an Arvon course to justify its usefulness.

If we were a healthy society, presumably we would not need to be schooled so deliberately into an understanding of the life of our own language – our society itself would supply the understanding naturally and fully in the flourishing use of our mother-tongue. But we have to admit our society fails there. Even such a minimal cultural essential as respect for literacy, and for the worlds of meaning that open within words, even so much as could be taken for granted in a nineteenth century Lancashire weaver, or a Welsh collier of fifty years ago, or a Scots shepherd, cannot any longer be left for our society to provide of itself, by its own initiative. It seems to me we now have to regard the body of our language as we might regard the deprived body of a man in prison: only a deliberate regimen of planned exercise will keep it going at all, let alone develop athletic prowess. Language is not so natural, even among such higher primates as we are. Whatever else we forget we should not forget that a man, deprived of all stimulation for about five days, forgets language.

Arvon has been a very conscious response to the crisis we have been talking about. And this book is an attempt to spread the response further, into schools and into the public at large, by the two men who first put Arvon together, and who have already given much of their lives to it.

RESPONSES

As will be evident from the range and variety of the preceding pieces, the original letter inviting sixteen writers to contribute to this celebration of John Moat and the work of Arvon allowed each writer complete freedom of choice as to the nature of their offering. However the letter did contain suggestions for possible lines of approach, including a list of questions about the nature of the writing process itself. Once the book began to come together, we decided to post these questions on a website and invite the wider Arvon community to respond to them. We were so delighted by the number, range and quality of the replies that a representative selection of them is included here in the hope that it might prove helpful to aspiring writers.

Because of considerations of space most of the following answers to each question have been edited for length, but all the responses can be found complete on the website at www.arvonwritingroom.org

Some of the authors of these replies are already published as poets, novelists or short-story writers. Some chose to identify themselves only by a forename or soubriquet, others to remain anonymous. In the following selection each respondent has been identified by initials. In forename alphabetical order their names are:

AK Anne Kenny

AV Alistair Valentine

BK Beryl Kingston

CA Claire Askew

CC Christos Callow Jr

CJA C J Allen

CoM 'courseofmirrors'

CW Charlie Wilson

DI Deborah Install

E Emma

EH Emily Hallewell

EL Emma Lee

EP Emma Page

JA Judy Astley

JC Jane Cooper

JG Juliet Greenwood

JP Jude Parker

JW Julia Webb

KD K Davis

KK Kate Kenworthy

KM Kim Moore

KMan Kevan Manwaring

LH Lorna Howarth

LP Lynne C Potter

M 'Mols'

MA Maggie Angles

MH Maggie How

ML Maxine Linnell

MN Marc Nash

NJD Neil John Dean

NW Noel Williams

PD Paul Deaton

PH Paul Houghton

PO 'Poetic Oxana'

PP Penny Portabella

PW Pete Walsh

R Rona

RM Roy Marshall

SA Safina Akram

SB Sarah Butler

SH Sam Hudson

WG 'Wrath of God'

ZB Zoe Broome

George Palmer of Arvon and Lorna Howarth of The Write Factor, who set up the website, are very grateful to all the writers who contributed to it, as is Lindsay Clarke who is responsible for this selection.

How does a book or piece of writing begin to take shape in your Imagination? Do you feel your writing is a process of inventing or discovering?

Endless dreaming, notes, freeform maps of characters and connections and story-shapes - talking to myself, as the characters, too - but underneath all that, barely at level of consciousness, is a theme which resonates profoundly with me, enough to compel me to keep exploring, keep inventing, keep nibbling at the edges until I find the best way to examine it and make it worth my time to write, and worth a reader's attention. **WG**

It usually begins with an unusual image or a string of them that have been captured in my notebooks. These images may come from the tail end of a dream or observations from real life. Hardy's notebooks are quite an inspiration. Equally though, a narrative may start with an intrusive or intriguing piece of dialogue – an utterance that has some urgency and mystery in it. These images and utterances are a given and have to be added to. This is where invention and discovery come in: from the fusion of the two. **PH**

There are two ways I write; the first is the logical, rational process, whereby I research, focus on what I wish to say consciously, and explicitly structure my work in advance. With an approximate idea of word count, key questions or ideas to be explored within the piece and a rough idea of how the work is going to be introduced, developed and finished. However, there is another second process and this is what I think of as being 'in the flow' or on automatic pilot. In this writing mode, it is almost as though I am not in charge and rather, the words just seem to flow. Passing from head, to fingers, to keys, and circumventing the mind. This second process, does not occur that often and ends up producing writing of a much higher calibre than the normal, logical, rational mode produces. **SA**

A story starts to tug at me at odd times until I listen to it. I think there's inventing *and* discovering involved, a strange process of unfolding the story as the characters form. The story comes from them. I have them speak, let them write letters, describe their childhoods, their hopes and fears. But I don't believe they 'take over'. It's up to me to make them who they are. They're probably all aspects of my own personality. **ML**

If the question had not given the option of discovery I would have said that invention is the catalyst of creativity. However, I believe my experience and imagination allow me to discover realms of possibility that invention alone would find wanting. **KD**

It's definitely a process of discovery. I'm a poet, and often the 'trigger' for a poem will just appear, unbidden. I'll suddenly hear a line in my head, or find a few snappy words stuck in there like an old tune. I put the trigger line or phrase on a piece of paper and then start poking around with it, building on it slowly. I think that's actually more like it: it's more like building than anything else. **CA**

Painful discovery! It's always about a character and it always starts with one particular moment in their life. **SH**

The idea appears in my head – no fanfare to announce it, no warning that I'm about to enter a creative flow – usually when I'm daydreaming. If I like the idea, I indulge it and let it meander about in my mind until there's some substance to it. It does rather feel like it has a life of its own at this point – so I sit back and watch, rather than trying to take over. **EH**

I think poetry is a form of relationship building, the means by which we can explore and understand the relationship we have with ourselves in the world, our life's journey. I think poets are people who have a strong, unavoidable desire to know this part of themselves; have to know it. Poetry is the quarrel with ourselves as Yeats said, it's a one to one relationship; the poet wants to know who she is and what she feels; the poems are her gift, they make the woods of life navigable, they provide life with its marker points, its recognisable trees, its truth and meaning. **PD**

I need a character first, rather than an idea, and often characters are reincarnations of people I have met along the course. Once the character begins to develop an identity, which often involves their own invented mythology, I do my usual What If - when the idea germinates, I research to decide: gender, setting, time frame etc. **PW**

What things trigger your imaginative process (for example, significant personal experiences, particular people, places, objects, dream imagery, myths, history, etc)?

I think for me the trigger is always based in a significant personal experience. Because it's personal, it's something I feel passionate about and that's what drives the story forward. The thing I have always loved about reading – especially as a young adult - has been the sharing of experience. It's that sudden understanding that someone else has felt that, and so it's okay. I'm not alone. **JG**

The idea of two characters colliding and the aftermath of that constantly fascinates me. I collect overhead snatches of conversation, I wonder about the person I see sitting across from me on the train, I latch onto anecdotes people tell, or things I read in the newspaper. Places are also really important in my fiction. My debut novel is set in London and I spent a lot of time walking around the city and mining my own experience of the place to create the atmosphere and detail I wanted for the novel. **SB**

For my second novel to form, I had to be confronted by the aggressive commuter, the silent colleague, the invisible housemate to recognize the wilful blindness all around me. To take a leap of imagination, everywhere I turned was to see books on quantum physics and parallel universes. The seal was attending a conference named 'The Spaces Between Us'. Suddenly all the particles flew into place and I had an idea and a title for a book. **PP**

I write best when I get out of my comfort zone – when I travel to somewhere completely new and a bit unknown, for example, or when something jolts me into uncomfortable territory. I write best when I'm unhappy, when I'm angry. I find that being happy means I write less, and when I do write I produce sweet, placid poems that don't take as many risks. **CA**

Prompts for stories have often come from free writing, so I see my subconscious as a huge well of resources. Other prompts are dreams, pictures or paintings – I am a very visual writer, so my imagination loves to take an image and play with it – it's the writing process that picks up the game and runs with it. Life-writing can turn into a fictional version – a story often seems to resonate with my readers if it reflects something I have actually experienced (write what you know), on the other hand, as mentioned above, some stories have come from paintings (especially Edward Hopper) and I have researched and invented stories (write what you don't know). **MH**

Most of all, what triggers my imaginative process is my reaction to life. For that, I need to live and to feel fully. Which is not always easy. Writing requires being completely exposed to myself, to others and to the world. Being vulnerable, allowing pain to come in is what makes true creativity possible. Readers know when they look at blood or at tomato sauce. When the impact with life is real, it will be able to touch the reader as well. **PO**

Although adding a scene "just because it really happened" is no guarantee that it'll be any good (lots of things "really" happen in life), I find that almost all my Imagination process is fired by real people, it gives me something solid to focus on while creating the subtext and characterization for them. **NJD**

Very often memory plays a significant part in my writing. I have written many poems which reflect my Irish ancestry, though I was born and brought up in England. It is as though I am trying to regain a mythical homeland. My writing is often very personal about places, parents (death and loss of memory) and being a parent (love, protectiveness and growing). It seems I need to write about what is emotionally most important to me. **AK**

I am deeply inspired by the landscape and its legends - the accretion of narrative which can build up around certain sites, especially ancient ones. As a professional storyteller - myths, fairy tales, folk tales are my stock-in-trade, and they all go into cauldron. I like to experience a place first hand - and this provides the grit in the oyster to my Imagination, as I stumble upon the telling details that make all the difference (details which no amount of print or web-based research will ever uncover). **KMan**

Many poems are triggered by interesting phrases or fragments, often without any sort of context. It's not unusual for these to set the poem going, and then be removed at some stage in the process. I'm prey to all the usual inspirations - childhood, relationships with parents and partner, love and death, place, nature and art. So when the starting point is so conventional, I'm often prompted to search for some different angle or insight - unfortunately, this may lead in directions which are interesting exercises, but not very authentic treatments of the subject. **NW**

How do you work – do you plan carefully or explore in the dark, trusting the process?

Planning for me will be about what to include, what to discard and also about making associations and beginning to see or make a shape or structure for writing. There may also be formal or technical issues that require some detailed planning. But I tend not to be happy with poems that end how I always thought they would as freshness and surprise are important. For this reason I have been experimenting with trying to write more freely and more quickly, sometimes very early in the morning, with not the merest whiff of a plan. **EP**

I start with a very rough plan, which I know is almost certainly going to change during the journey of the writing the novel. At this point I usually know the beginning and the end and a little in between. Then I start and it all changes. I find the more experience I have gained the more I have learnt to trust the process, and that it IS a process. I like the freedom to explore in the first draft of a book. Once I know the characters and the plot and where I'm going, then I sit down and plan more carefully. **JG**

I think myself into the heads and under the skin of all my main characters and quite a lot of the minor ones, using method acting techniques, until they are as familar as old friends. Then I work out exactly what is going to happen to them and when and what the results will be and do as much research as is needful. **BK**

A certain degree of planning is essential, even if it's only in the head: short stories can sit in the head quite well, but novels are another matter – that feat of architecture needs girders and ramparts. I think it's usually imperative to have a feasible framework but good to go with the process too, to surprise, delight, amuse and horrify yourself – in the hope that this experience will be successfully transmitted to the reader. **PH**

I remember working with Michele Roberts when I did my MA at UEA in Norwich. She would talk about the joy of writing into the dark, arguing that if you plan everything to the last detail then the writing process becomes dull and predictable. The more experienced I get, the more I subscribe to that view. I like to set off with a bit of an idea about the direction I'm heading in, and the people who'll be accompanying me, but I find it easier to root out the heart of my story and the reality of my characters by just sitting down and writing, and seeing what comes. **SB**

I often know where I want to end, and I always know where to start. The middle bit seems to unfurl like a roll of carpet in front of me as I go - so long as I keep writing, it keeps being written. **JC**

I wish I could plan carefully but the only planning that I have ever managed is to never be more than six feet from a notebook. **M**

I plan very, very carefully. As a book editor, I see a stark difference between the planned books and those written without any thought for structure and direction. **CW**

I like to plan a certain amount. I like to know the point I am trying to make and broadly what I would like the story arc to be. However I often find that things make a slight - or not so slight - change of direction, and I have to be willing to trust the process enough to at least see where that road is going. **DI**

I write fresh from my brain without careful planning. Planning and research either comes naturally or in later drafts, for example, historical research is planned in before from discoveries made for personal interest reasons, events naturally occur and influence my writing and choice of form comes later as I shape and draft the poem. **ZB**

Do you feel in control of your writing or are you responsive to the requirements of the work as it unfolds?

I quite like feeling NOT in complete control. That way there are those wonderful days when the work is flying and I end up absolutely elated by it all. Of course that's countered by times when I wonder if I'll ever write another coherent sentence. **JA**

I never feel in control of a long piece of fiction (i.e a novel). For a short story, especially a commissioned story, I'm more confident that I can achieve the word limit almost exactly and still do what I want to do. I'm more comfortable writing at speed, in short form, than at length, over months, when doubts creep in to overcome enthusiasm and confidence. **WG**

False dilemma. I am the work and the worker, I am in control and under control. I am unable to tell the difference. **CC**

When I write I feel as if I enter "flow" or move "into the zone" where my surroundings fall away and my focus is solely on the writing itself. Therefore, I'd have to say I'm responsible to the requirements of the work as it unfolds. **EL**

There's some control but some surprises. It can feel a bit like taking a very inquisitive terrier out for a walk. **JC**

I never feel in control. I do not know where the ideas have come from. Looking back over past work, I am surprised and sometimes startled, wondering what prompted the poem or story and to what depths I have delved in the search for inspiration. **LP**

Both. I think being in control of an artwork is being able to be responsive. I couldn't imagine writing a work that I had planned out every chapter, every scene of which character was interacting with which others. For me that would emerge as a very arid work. I'm not saying that people can't write with such control, just that I know I couldn't. **MN**

When a piece of writing is going well there is a point at which my sense of being in control and my need to respond to the requirements of the unfolding work are in perfect balance. This state of mind is wonderful and unforgettable. It produces a feeling of excitement and calm in a sort of perfect cocktail. **RM**

It controls me at first, I then catch up to it, wrestle it to the ground, then control it!! **NJD**

There's an oceanic feeling as I set out – it's like paddling across the

Pacific, with only the sextant of my craft to guide my. I'm at the mercy of strange tides and I have to be careful not to be blown completely off course. I embrace this negative capability – the belly of the whale – and see it as an essential part of the creative process. Illumination comes with hindsight. So, the first time around, I'm groping in the dark; the second time – it's writing with the lights on. **KMan**

Do you write a first draft quickly and then revise it or build carefully from the start?

Build carefully. I can't move on until I've got the previous chapter 'right'. **E**

I tend to under-write quickly and have to push to get to the end of a long piece. If I pick at what's already been written too early, I can get bogged down. Then I have to fill the writing out, help it make sense and hang together. Reading sections at my writers' group is invaluable to show me where I'm not being clear enough. **ML**

Every new para or chunk of work requires to be lined up with what came before it in order to be sure about what will come after it - a constant process of revision. Not sure this is sane, right, etc - but it's how I do it... in a short story that can be quite easy; in a novel, it's like turning a huge cargo vessel in a troubled sea, inch by inch... **WG**

I build it carefully. But this is partly because I don't start at page 1 and plod gamefully or painfully on until I can write 'The end' and feel relieved. I write any scene I fancy whenever I fancy it and then stitch sequences together. That way I don't get bored, I enjoy what I'm doing and I don't write padding. If I find any when I'm stitching it gets zapped out. **BK**

My opinion is: Write quickly, revise, yes, but not redraft, and never do editing while writing, it's suicide! Writing and editing must be done separately, because self-editing – usually having a tendency to self-censorship – delays and occasionally ruins the creative process. Judge your work after you finish it, not while creating it. **CC**

Build carefully from the start. I prefer the process of writing to the editing/revision stage so the fewer edits and revisions I have to do the better. **EL**

I revise all the time; every line or sentence gets written and re-written as I go. I do edit afterwards, but I don't go in for huge re-drafts. One day I'd like to write a novel, and I'm sure that will need a very different sort of approach. **JC**

I allow the ideas to flow onto the page, rarely backtracking until I reach a natural conclusion or my writing runs out of steam. If I think too hard, the creative juices dry up and I start to agonise over every apostrophe and split infinitive. Once finished, I leave it for a few days before returning to decide whether it is worthwhile. If it is, I spend a long time reviewing and refining it. I always read my work aloud to myself to listen to the flow and the sense. **LP**

Few poems fall perfectly formed out of the sky and onto the page. All writing really is re-writing, isn't it? **CJA**

I write a first draft as quickly as it allows me to, which is sometimes not very quickly, although I use some devices to try and get a whole draft down in one sitting if I can. For example, rather than find the exact word or phrase at each point, I'll insert a "placeholder", which does the job approximately, and mark it as such to remind myself in revision that this was not a choice made, but rather a query to be addressed. **NW**

On my first draft, I always go by the rule 'don't get it right, get it written'. Once I have a full draft written - that's when the real writing begins. **KMan**

How do you deal with blocks in the writing process?

I write. It doesn't matter what. Any old rubbish will do. I find if I keep on tapping out the words on the keyboard (banning Facebook and Twitter first) eventually the writing will begin to flow and I'll be back on track again. Then I go back and delete the rubbish. Except sometimes I find on reading it again that it wasn't that bad, after all. **JG**

I sometimes let them happen as a fallow time where new aspects can surface, but I'm not a great believer in writer's block. When I have a deadline, I meet it. So when there's no deadline there's no excuse. But I still procrastinate and put everything else in life first. Sometimes I realise how important a break is and come back to the process fresh. **ML**

I ask myself the question: what is it about this that makes you afraid, or uncomfortable – and I listen for the answers. Sometimes the answer is: 'I don't know how to say/write it right' (and I tell myself to just say it, make it better later). Sometimes the answer is: 'I'm tired/feel ill/need a break to dream about this' and then I let myself drift a while, and return in a few hours or days. **WG**

Do something else entirely. It could be another writing project-in-progress (e.g. an article or review) or it could be painting the bathroom, fixing the garden, or going on a long walk for a good blast of air. Usually it's just overload or anxiety and will pass. You have to do something else – let the blocked project breathe for a while and come back to it fresh. If there's no drastic deadline I think a few days away from it can be a good thing. **PH**

Starting out, I suffered. I didn't appreciate that you move in and out of states as a writer. You are not solely a writer in that you put words on a page. You are a dreamer, a theorist, a philosopher. The mastery comes from accepting when it is time of one role over another and when that role has overstayed its welcome. **PP**

There are no blocks, only excuses. **CC**

If the block is that I've started a piece of work but can't see how to continue or end it, I know I've written myself into a dead end and need to go back to take the piece in a different direction. If the paper is blank and it's not down to pressure to write something but more of a case of stage fright because I don't know whether an idea will work or how a piece of work will be received, I remind myself that you can't edit a blank piece of paper. It's a sign the inner critic needs silencing as you cannot write and critique what you're writing at the same time. The two processes are different. **EL**

Easy! Just get going! Think of it as a formula one race track and having a series of minor near misses that you can clean up later. If in doubt get thoroughly pissed on one single glass of brandy so that your mind relaxes. **AV**

If I feel uninspired, I leave it and move onto something else, hoping that in the dark reaches of the night a new idea or an alternative direction will pop unbidden into my mind. **LP**

I accept there are all manner of limiting circumstances, the weather, the moon, the needs of friends, my body's metabolism, the wavelength I tune into. Sometimes, when I bang at a door too long, get exhausted and give up, the mind suddenly clears. **CoM**

Do you write in service of any particular values?

I don't write in service of values, that might seem like teaching or preaching, and I can't bear that as a reader! But I do hold strong and long-explored values and intentions in life, so my writing must speak from them, reflect them in some way. I'm trying to write honestly about life and human predicaments. **ML**

That's a difficult one. I am not guided by any higher religious or political ideals. My main object is to be true to the poem - that is that the poem doesn't have to be true (as in relating a true event as it happened) but it has to feel true to the reader - a kind of universal truth I guess if that makes any sense. I am also in service to the idea of refining one's art - I want to be the best writer that I can be. There is always something more to be learned. **JW**

Yes. Do these values belong in a certain category? No. My most important value is that writing is world-changing (to the extent that that is possible). I am also not interested in supporting commonplace or currently popular ideas. I hate easy values, I think that the most important truths are the hardest to accept. **CC**

Only that each piece should be the best it can be according to the aims of the individual piece. I much prefer to write a piece that explores a topic and gives readers space to draw their own conclusions or read my writing in accordance with their own moral values. I don't want to tell readers what to think, but I don't self-censor and avoid taboo subjects. **EL**

That made me pause for thought! I guess I value Imagination and creativity as much as our illustrious language (I love the sound, look and feel of words) so attempt to promote those. I value mythology and fairytales and believe they are a necessity so have become an advocate for fantasy writing. I raise my boys with moral values but will encourage them to make up their own minds on their beliefs. **KD**

Accessibility. I teach Literature 101 to young people from backgrounds where books just do not factor into people's lives. These are readers who find the very idea of the written word frightening. Yet, when I introduce them to a poet whose goal is openness and understanding – someone like Billy Collins – they suddenly get it. And they want to read it, and they want to write. **CA**

I hope there's a basic humanity underlying my poetry. By which I mean I'd like to think of it as compassionate and at least aspiring to an intelligent and thoughtful view of the world and the human condition. I want to honour and respect the gift of language too. If it's possible, I want to write something that is true and beautiful. **CJA**

I think all writers are unable to keep underlying values out of their work. One of the values explored in my case is the importance of family connection and continuity between generations, for better or worse. **RM**

I write in service of particular values. These values are: life - first and foremost. Its diversity, its richness, its abundance - are all the things that I feel people should be reminded of. Other values that I promote are: creativity itself, as the highest manifestation of humanity; celebration of loving relationships between people; social justice; care for Mother Earth. **PO**

The only god is authenticity: the truth of an experience, the truth of a character, of a voice, of a sentence. **KMan**

What have you learned from the practice of your craft?

I've learnt that writing – like anything creative you strive to do well - is a process. A long, hard process. Frustrating at times, but when it's zinging and you're in the zone it's the most amazing feeling on earth. Better than sex. Better even than chocolate. **JG**

That I have to be able to trust that I'm a good enough writer and that the story is good enough to hold the reader. If I didn't believe in those two precepts, I'd be paralysed. **E**

That the learning and practice of the craft never ends and far from being frustrating, this is what makes it exciting. It's very satisfying to write a good sentence. If there's enough of these in a sound structure you hope they will form a good story or novel. Nevertheless, it's a life long process. **PH**

So much. I have learned let in all the senses. To move between the hemispheres of human experience – the mental, emotional, material, physical, sensual and practical. To not give one too much sway. I have learned what it is to breathe in and out in life. **PP**

That reading and writing and sharing poetry has power in it. Poetry is often misunderstood by those who've never really dealt with it – people think it's archaic and serves no purpose. This isn't true. Poetry is what language was made for. Get struggling students to write poems and their literacy scores will sky-rocket, as will their social skills. Poetry is not old-fashioned, doesn't have to be self-aggrandising or dull. I've learned that none of the rumours are true. Poetry is seriously hip, and what's more, it's a long way from being dead. **CA**

That writing keeps me sane. I do it every day one way or another. **KK**

To let go of fear – fear of failing, fear of looking daft, fear of life being too short to write all I want to write. And to value all writing. Even the pieces you don't like. Because it's only by giving yourself permission to write material that's not amazing that you gain the courage and the freedom to write the stuff you're proud of. **CW**

That writing poetry can often seem like a rather complicated way of being ignored, but somehow, despite that, it's not showing any signs of going away. I'm sure this has something to do with poetry's relationship to the deep roots of language. **CJA**

Skills of sharpening what seeks expression. Orchestration of suspense, the chiming word, a rhythm that engages. **CoM**

Through writing I have learnt patience and tolerance and also that you can't please all of the people all of the time - so don't try. I have learnt that there is a wonderful world floating around in my mind and if I take the trouble to stop and listen occasionally I can learn a lot from myself as well as others. **R**

To be humble - there are always people further along the way than you, to learn from, admire, subvert and assassinate. To be determined, disciplined, unsentimental and austere. A lot of writing is simply about what to cut back, what to leave out. I have become adept at murdering darlings. **KMan**

What is the relationship between the writer's imagination and that of the reader?

The biggest lesson I've learnt is understanding that the reader's imagination is different from mine. I see my story so vividly in my own mind – I live it, in fact – that I can't see that a reader will come at the novel from quite a different direction. From their own life, their own imagination and their own experiences. That, I've finally learnt, is where an editor comes in. A really good editor is an intermediary between the writer and the reader. She'll spot the things that might not make sense to the reader, or might inadvertently alienate them from the book. And when the book is done, and it goes out into the world, then, as a writer, you have to let go. It's not your child any longer: it has a life of its own. **JG**

The writer has a duty to describe what he or she sees in their mind's eye so that it can be taken up and shaped by the reader's Imagination. **E**

The product of the writer's Imagination is what speaks to the reader through the poem. The writer needs to give the reader recognisable anchors to hold onto and then the sky is the limit. **JW**

It is the interface where the story happens. **KMan**

Symbiotic - but the beauty of using words rather than any other media is that the reader can use their imagination to enrich the world you have created. How brilliant is that! **MA**

I love this question. It is a concert. You, the conductor, do not turn to your audience at the end of the performance and take your bows. Oh no. Your audience wants to know what it is to be the violinist – to be the violin – to be the percussionists. Your relationship to them is to read their needs and lead them through the heights and the depths of the orchestra. You move them inside the instruments and the musicians and move them out again. You move them into a state of being. They paint the rest. **PP**

Writers are here to tell people what they may not want to hear, in such a wonderful way that they will listen. The writer's existence is justified by the mental effort to imagine/conceive of ideas, images, emotions, worlds, etc, that most wouldn't (or couldn't) think of. It doesn't end in imagining the unimaginable though – the hardest part is translating it in human language (which is where poetry comes in). **CC**

When, as a reader, I really connect with a writer's work, it's not like a conversation – it's deeper than that. It's almost like a hive-mind. A good writer puts me in their character's skin and lets me see, hear and feel what's happening. As a teacher of creative writing I utterly hate the command, "show, don't tell," and ban it from my classrooms. But that command is heading in the right direction – writers shouldn't just tell the reader something. The reader should come out of the other end of a great piece of writing feeling changed. Don't tell them, don't show them – change them. Maybe that's it. **CA**

Writing and reading are, for me, parts of the same activity; one completes the other in a sort of metaphysical handshake. Schopenhauer said something along the lines of 'Reading is thinking with someone else's brain.' But when it comes to poetry those thoughts can and will expand and ramify in the mind of the reader. And in a way I think that's what poetry is supposed to do. **CJA**

I think a poem offers a kind of map or sketch of an area that a reader is at liberty to follow or fill in as much as she desires. The writer has to imagine the thing as fully as possible, but on the understanding that the reader will imagine something else. What we're doing in poetry is making something out of our experience to give readers a new experience, which they can then make something else out of. **NW**

Do writers have any moral responsibility in their work wider than fidelity to their personal vision?

I would not personally write material that was exploitative, racist, sexist, ageist, pornographic, intended to encourage hatred or violence - but I will and do write about those subjects in ways which, I hope, examine the consequences for those who are affected by those issues, or by those who espouse them. **WG**

No. It's when writing subverts expectation that it gets exciting. **E**

The personal vision should be enough because it cannot help but represent that writer's moral framework. Once its disseminated not everyone will agree with it – as should be. We need a broad panoply of voices and visions. **PH**

That's a difficult question as it inevitably leads onto self censorship. Values change too. Books once considered immoral, now are lauded as classics. The only way to proceed is to be true to yourself, your own moral compass. **JP**

If a poem retains an inherent integrity then I think it can look beyond personal vision in the language chosen and the situations / issues described, but I still think that ultimately, a poem has to be sufficient unto itself - stand firm without props, even if also precarious. **MA**

As part of the society, writers are responsible for that society's future, possibly more than most people. In the past, the writer's dream wasn't to have their novel adapted to a Hollywood movie – in many cases, it was to help start a revolution of some sort, social, intellectual or even emotional (personal). Writers are world-changers or they are wankers. I believe that any work of art not created to make the world better (or at least, more beautiful) has insufficient justification for its existence. **CC**

It really depends whether the writer intends to publish the work. Personal writing needs to strip away responsibilities and rules and allow the freedom to be selfish and express darker aspects of the self in a safe medium. But writing that's for others to read is different. Just as you consider what you say verbally to other people, you have to reflect on the impact of your words on the reader, the power of your work to carry opinions that affect and change a reader. Awareness, respect and empathy are key. **CW**

I've not encountered a social structure, a faith, a political system or party, an institutional mission or ethos, or any social system which seems to me flexible enough, humane enough, or, indeed, coherent enough to warrant unquestioning service from artists. The responsibility of the artist is to test all such systems: not necessarily to resist, as such, though this may be desirable, but simply to explore it, to push its boundaries, to question. But I don't think poems need to have a political agenda as such to do such things: the poet simply has to be prepared to say whatever needs to be said, irrespective of who is discomfited by it. I guess this is the poet as Fool, in a certain sense, and the duty may be no more than to reflect back to readers the world they've created and the ways they live in it. I think it is also the responsibility of the poet to seek the spiritual in art, although I'd want to say "spiritual" with the lowest emphasis I can get away with. It seems to me that religion tends to abuse genuine spiritual experience, by which I mean the numinous, the liminal, the intensity of experience which most people seem to experience but find it hard to articulate, by codifying it. It seems to me that poetry can still express and represent such experience without deceit - both the uncertainties and the splendours of contemporary understanding of the world. **NW**

Perhaps a writer's moral responsibility is to themselves and the story they feel compelled to tell. Even the bleakest story reveals something of the human condition. I was motivated to set up The Write Factor by John Moat's words that "The unique story you have to tell is essential to the completion of the all-inclusive story of the Universe." **LH**

Yes, to this planet we call home and all beings upon it. To the canon of literature and to their community - physical, intentional, ecological). No writer is an island. We're all involved in this ongoing project called Creation, whatever we perceive its cause. What we choose to bring into it as an act of highest moral responsibility. **KMan**

Afterthought: John Moat

UNFINISHED BUSINESS...

THE QUESTION AS to whether Arvon was an Arts or an Education project was never discussed by the writers involved in its initial venturing. In fact I guess the idea that there must be division between the two appeared to them, even as it would today, simply evidence of a society that employs arbitrary divisions to create the competing territories, the little hierarchies and guarded cash-pots that enable a dysfunctional bureaucratic system to go about its business. If from the outset it seemed obvious for Arvon to suggest itself to schools and colleges and, perhaps most obvious of all, teacher-training colleges, maybe this was because much of what originally impelled John Fairfax and myself was a furious feeling of how our time at school would have been freed into life had there been the opportunity we were fetched later – the encounter and chance to work with actual poets.

From the start we were struck by how many teacher-trainees were gifted, and who when provided with the Arvon licence to explore and work with their Imagination discovered not only new possibility for their own fulfilment, but an extended view of the authority they might bring to their teaching. And so it was brought home to us how vast in the national context was the educational resource which, because not acknowledged by the system, was being effectively proscribed, or held

211

dormant, unrealised – depriving not just the teachers themselves, and inevitably their students, but the entire nation of part of its essential life.

With the increasing demands of the syllabus and the politically imposed targets for examination grades, the situation has simply grown more dire. Most teachers are so depleted by what the system demands of them – in largely formulaic teaching that will produce the standard grades, and in vacuous administration – that it is unreal to suppose they could find time or energy to foster their own self-expressive, imaginative lives. The consequence is predictable enough – teachers come to view the Imagination not as a reality in their own lives, but as some technical application that can be ear-marked and graded by the system. As a result they are often taken out of their depth by the raw, unruly Imagination of their students, are perhaps intimidated, and haven't the experience to either encourage or discipline it. No wonder one hears of how many are under stress, and feel demoralised and that they are unvalued by society.

At some point in the 1990s John Fairfax and I were invited to run a 5-day course for teachers. It was held in mid-August which, the teachers told us, was providential: a week earlier and they'd have been still too exhausted from the load of the last school-year; a week later and they'd already be preparing for the next. John and I were shaken by watching how in five days, given simply the opportunity and the confidence to give way to the Imagination, they... well what can I say, they seemed like those miracle Chinese paper fragments which placed in water unfurl into flowers – they or maybe it was the famous 'child within' seemed to wake... to excitement and self-belief. And perhaps more telling, to eagerness to share this excitement with their students on their return to the 'chalk-face'.

There seemed no option but to see if anything could be made from what the course had so clearly demonstrated. We brought together a group of teachers, writers and education officers under Lawrence Sail's chairmanship and funded by South West Arts. We agreed to set up a pilot project, a programme of practical arts and crafts workshops where teachers could, with the guidance of practising artists and crafts people, develop their own creative work in a range of disciplines. We called the project Tandem, wanting to infer that here was a meeting of two complementary professions, and so distance it from the usual 'artists-in-schools' schemes aimed exclusively at the students, and which may even further undermine the confidence of teachers by implication they are simply not up to coping either with their own or their students' imaginative work.

Was it a success? Much of it was. Some of the events were unforgettable, and it created sufficient response to warrant funding for a well-produced Evaluation Report. Had Tandem been able to follow the way of Arvon's gradual long-term development, allowing its resonance and the case for further funding to build on repeated proof of its experience, then maybe it could similarly have established itself – but ultimately there wasn't the energy to sustain it, and the essential funding prospects were compromised by its coinciding with a vastly funded Arts Council initiative, Creative Partnerships. On the face of it Creative Partnerships was a larger scale and more efficiently administered means of achieving all that Tandem hoped to develop – but fundamentally they were at odds. That Creative Partnerships was closely aligned with the 'big picture' utilitarian concerns of the Education System was clear from the Prospectus: "...designed to develop the skills of children and young people across England, raising their aspirations, achievements and life chances." Whereas the emphasis of Tandem's concern was with education that primarily addressed individual fulfilment; one that enabled individuals through some form of imaginative self-expression to discover, develop and own their unique capacities, and to see this as the true-to-life path to integrated society. For me, two quotations we profiled on the front cover of the Report were proof that the project had succeeded. From one of the artists involved: "This Tandem opportunity to work with teachers, and so be engaged in education, is like the fulfilment of one aspect of my vocation." And from a teacher: "Tandem is the first initiative I've come across that recognises the centrality of teachers' creativity to their role in education."

But before we were off the hook we were struck by another possibility – that of a way to help redress what at the time was being seen as a crisis in teachers' sense of self-worth by celebrating the often unacknowledged success of so many in identifying, affirming, nurturing and mentoring the gifts of individual students. We conceived of a countywide festival and schools programme in which the lead participants would be from among all those who attributed their success to the inspiration and encouragement of a particular teacher. So the festival was to be called, *That Teacher* – and there came a wealth of ideas for how it might extend to the creative involvement of schools, teachers and students. Conceived as a way to enlarge on the festival was the publication of a book, also titled *That Teacher* – a collection of the memories of people with conspicuous careers describing their indebtedness to the guidance and encouragement of the one teacher. But in the end the funding we were counting on wasn't granted, and we were forced to concede the idea must be shelved.

In 1990, long before Tandem, John Lane, a trustee of Dartington Hall, half-jokingly invited me to suggest a use for a wonderful building currently empty on the Dartington estate. The school it had housed had closed and it was waiting to be put to new purpose. I had recently been in touch with Thomas Brooman, the then Director of WOMAD. I rang him with an idea, and soon the pair of us, together with David Pease,

Arvon's National Director, were at a meeting with Dartington Trustees. The idea was to set up a national laboratory, an intensive generator, a reactor for the Imagination. This would specifically be a place to which teachers would come and, Arvon-wise, spend time exploring their own creative excitement guided and animated by visiting artists – from any of the imaginative arts, including the creative sciences. One need only imagine the World musicians that WOMAD might have drawn to the venture to glimpse our excitement. It was because we had seen how on Arvon courses teachers coming alive to their own driving Imagination would feel suddenly they had now authority to work with their student's Imagination, that we could imagine how such a centre could be catalytic, a pivotal resource in extending and nurturing creative education… across the country.

I don't think I ever fully understood why after initial enthusiasm the idea foundered – particularly since we were all agreed it would be a likely candidate for funding from a wide range of sources. It could have been that Dartington sensed a cuckoo was out to lay in its nest. But somehow the heart went out of the idea. The *particular* idea, but not the vision. My reason for writing this may be helplessly subjective. I never lose the feeling that what we glimpsed at Dartington wasn't aside from Arvon, but a natural extension to, even the completion of the Arvon enterpise. And that because, in my estimate, it would now be a direct, timely and fully-focused benefit to a society and its way of education which being out of touch with the cardinal Imagination had lost their way. It seemed at the time to be so available as to be almost a thing given, and having experienced the accidents and charmed encounters and the unlikely providence that had made Arvon possible, I couldn't understand why this new dimension didn't likewise fall into place!

I have to say I still lie restless some nights, and remember my old mentor, Edmond Kapp, telling me fiercely, "An idea not acted on remains a property of the mind alone…" and then I'm wondering did we, did I, ever adequately pursue the idea? So that's what this was for, to have at least left a marker. Let providence find someone – say someone who has just been fetched the three Gold Bars in the 'literary lottery' – who'll do themselves a favour, pick it up… and run with it.

THE CONTRIBUTORS

IN ORDER OF APPEARANCE:

Sir Andrew Motion has published many award-winning volumes of verse, fiction, biography and criticism. He was Poet Laureate from 1999 to 2009 and is a Patron of Arvon.

John Moat has published many volumes of verse and several novels, most recently *A Fabrication of Gold* (The Write Factor, 2011), and is a regular contributor to *Resurgence Magazine* under the pseudonym Didymus. He is also a painter, peace activist, environmentalist and educator who has set up a number of charities including Yarner Trust, Tandem and the Extension Trust. With his friend John Fairfax he co-founded Arvon.

Carol Ann Duffy is the present Poet Laureate and is a Patron of Arvon. She has published many volumes of verse and her work has won several awards. *Miles Away* was first published in *Selling Manhattan* (Anvil Press 1987), and *Moniack Mhor* in *The Bees* (Picador 2009). Both poems are reprinted with permission.

Jules Cashford writes and lectures on Mythology and the Imagination. She is the author of *The Moon: Myth and Image* (Cassell Illustrated, 2003), a translation of *The Homeric Hymns* (Penguin Classics, 2003), and is co-author of *The Myth of the Goddess: Evolution of an Image*, (Penguin, 1993). She has made two films on Jan van Eyck.

Alice Oswald lives in Devon and is married with three children. She has published six books of poetry and two anthologies. Her most recent book, *Memorial* (Faber, 2011) is a re-imagining of Homer's *Iliad*.

Seamus Heaney is a poet and Nobel Laureate and also a Patron of Arvon. *Visitations* is a revised version of an essay which appeared earlier under the title *Apt Admonishment* in *The Hudson Review*, Vol LXI, No 1.

Andrew Miller attended an Arvon course in 1979 when Angela Carter and Elaine Feinstein were the tutors and Alan Sillitoe the visiting mid-week writer. He is the author of six novels. His most recent, *Pure* (Hodder & Stoughton, 2011), won the 2011 Costa Book of the Year award. He is a Visiting Fellow at Bath Spa University.

Adam Thorpe was born in Paris in 1956, and began his professional career as a mime. He is the author of ten novels, including *Ulverton* (Vintage, 1998) and *Hodd* (Jonathan Cape, 2009), two collections of stories and six books of poetry, the latest being *Voluntary* (Jonathan Cape), a Poetry Book Society Recommendation. His translation of Flaubert's *Madame Bovary* appeared in 2011 with Vintage Classics. His most recent novel, *Flight* (Cape), was published this year.

(Editor's addendum: Readers may like to know that in 2001, Adam inherited responsibility for the Phoenix Press from John Fairfax and John Moat, to whom it had been passed on in the 1960s by George and Kit Barker, who started it with Morris Carpenter in the 1930s. A truly golden chain! Adam renamed it Grand Phoenix Press in 2001 to distinguish it from the Orion imprint. He produced eight pamphlets seven of them letterpress-printed, "before impecuniousness stalled the enterprise.")

Lawrence Sail is a freelance writer. He has published eleven collections of poems, most recently *Waking Dreams: New & Selected Poems* (Bloodaxe Books, 2010: Poetry Book Society Special Commendation) and *Songs of the Darkness: Poems for Christmas* (Enitharmon Press, 2010). *Sift: Memories of Childhood* (Impress Books) also appeared in 2010. He was chairman of Arvon from 1990 to 1994.

Lindsay Clarke is the author of seven novels including *The Chymical Wedding* (Jonathan Cape, 1989), which won the Whitbread Award for Fiction, and more recently *The Water Theatre* (Alma Books, 2010), which was long-listed for the Impac Dublin International Literary Award.

Colette Bryce is a poet and editor. Originally from Derry, N. Ireland, she now lives in the North East of England. An Arvon course at Lumb Bank in 1992 provided her with a doorway into writing, and she has been involved ever since as a student and as a tutor. Her three collections are published by Picador and she received the Cholmondeley Award for her poetry in 2010. 'The Poetry Bug' is from *Self-Portrait in the Dark* (Picador, 2008), and 'The White Page' is unpublished in book form.

Patrick Harpur has written a history of the Imagination, *The Philosophers' Secret Fire* (Penguin 2002) and, most recently, the rather ambitiously-titled, *A Complete Guide to the Soul* (Rider Books, 2010). He is also responsible for the alchemical revelations of *Mercurius; or, the Marriage of Heaven and Earth* (Squeeze Press, 2008).

Linda Proud's novels – *The Botticelli Trilogy* and its prequel, *A Gift for the Magus* (Godstow Press) – are inspired by Neoplatonic themes but she herself follows the (concordant) philosophy of Advaita Vedanta. She is co-founder with her husband, David Smith, of Godstow Press.

Nick Stimson is a freelance playwright and theatre director. His work includes: 'NHS The Musical' with music by Jimmy Jewell; 'A Winter's Tale' with music and lyrics by Howard Goodall; 'Who Ate All The Pies?' with music by Jimmy Jewell; 'Hello, Mister Capello'; 'Korczak' with music by Chris Williams; 'Promised Land' with Anthony Clavane; 'Midas' with music by Jimmy Jewell; and 'Cornish Phoenix' with music by Chris Williams. He is currently working on a new play for the Theatre Royal Plymouth based on the work of the artist Beryl Cook. Nick has also published two collections of poetry; *In Magnet Air* (Phoenix Press); and *Flying Pigs* (Enitharmon).

Penelope Shuttle is a poet and author, widow of Peter Redgrove (1932-2003). Her most recent publication is *Sandgrain And Hourglass* (Bloodaxe Books, October 2010), a Recommendation of The Poetry Book Society. *Unsent: New And Selected Poems* 1980-2012 appears from Bloodaxe Books in October 2012. She was born in Middlesex but has lived in Cornwall since 1970. She knew Totleigh Barton in its pioneer days, and continues to tutor for Arvon.

Maggie Gee has written a writer's memoir, *My Animal Life* (Telegram, 2010) a collection of short stories, *The Blue* (Telegram, 2007), and eleven novels including *The White Family, My Cleaner* and *My Driver*, all published by Telegram. She loves Arvon, and it has transformed the novel she is writing, *Virginia Woolf in Manhattan*.

Monique Roffey is a Trinidadian-born British writer. Her second novel *The White Woman on the Green Bicycle* (Simon & Schuster, 2009) received widespread critical acclaim and was shortlisted for the Orange Prize 2010 and the Encore prize 2011. Her other novels include *sun dog* (Scribner, 2002) and *Archipelago* (out in July 2012). Her erotic memoir, *With the Kisses of his Mouth* (Simon & Schuster) was published to much praise and controversy in the summer of 2011. She has a PhD in Creative Writing and teaches regularly for Arvon, the Writer's Lab in Skyros and on the MA at Goldsmiths. She is currently an RLF Fellow at Greenwich University.

Satish Kumar is the editor of *Resurgence Magazine*, Founder and Director of Programmes at Schumacher College an international centre for ecological studies, and of The Small School in Hartland, North Devon. His most notable accomplishment is a 'peace walk' to the capitals of four nuclear-armed countries – Washington, London, Paris and Moscow – a trip of over 8,000 miles. He insists that reverence for nature should be at the heart of every political and social debate. He is the author of an autobiography, *No Destination*, of *You Are Therefore I Am: A Declaration of Dependence*, and of *The Buddha and the Terrorist* all published by Green Books.

Ted Hughes OM (1930 – 1998) was a poet and author of many children's books and critical essays. He was Poet Laureate from 1984 until his death. His widow, **Carol Hughes**, is a Patron of Arvon.

A Fabrication of Gold, Welcombe Overtures and *100 Poems* by John Moat are available from www.thewritefactor.co.uk